Child Protection
AND EAR
YEARS WO

College,

1

JENNIE LINDON

Hodder & Stoughton
A MEMBER OF THE HODDER HEADLINE GROUP

Orders: please contact Bookpoint Ltd, 78 Milton Park, Abingdon, Oxon OX14 4TD. Telephone: (44) 01235 827720, Fax: (44) 01235 400454. Lines are open from 9.00 - 6.00, Monday to Saturday, with a 24 hour message answering service. Email address: orders@bookpoint.co.uk

British Library Cataloguing in Publication Data
A Catalogue record for this title is available from The British Library

ISBN 0-340-70558-2

First published 1998

Impression number	10 9 8 7 6 5 4 3
Year	2005 2004 2003 2002 2001 2000

Typeset by Wearset, Boldon, Tyne and Wear
Printed in Great Britain for Hodder & Stoughton Educational, a division of Hodder Headline Plc, 338 Euston Road, London NW1 3BH by J. W. Arrowsmith Ltd., Bristol.

Dedication

To my parents, from whom I experienced respect and such very good care.
To my son and daughter, who continue to teach me about being a parent.

Contents

Acknowledgements

I appreciate how much I have learned from conversations with children, early years workers, other fellow-professionals and parents. In particular, I would like to thank Fiona Becker from the NSPCC Training Unit in Leicester; Liz Cowley, formerly Senior Development Officer at the Early Childhood Unit; and Kathy Forbes of Buckinghamshire Social Services. I learned a great deal about the legal process in court by running joint workshops on the Children Act 1989 with local authority solicitors – particular thanks to those in Croydon and Lewisham.

The photographs were taken at the Pen Green Centre for the Under 5s and their families, Corby; many thanks to Margy Whalley for granting permission to reproduce the images.

All the examples and case studies were developed from real people and places. In every case I have changed the names of children or adults and any other details that could break confidentiality.

Introduction

Child protection is an important aspect of good practice in all early years settings. Yet the contribution of workers in early years care, education and playwork has often been overlooked in guidelines on child abuse. This book is written especially for early years workers and provides the knowledge and understanding to help you develop a positive role with children, parents and other professionals.

The book explains how your responsibilities fit into the broader system of child protection and describes how awareness of possible child abuse can shape your work with individual children and groups. Staff in nurseries, preschools, children's centres or after-school clubs all have an important role to play in protection and prevention. The chapters of the book cover information and advice that will help you to establish good practice and increase your awareness of what you are already doing that can support effective child protection.

Chapter 1 places the current approach to child protection in its context through a description of the historical background. The chapter then moves on to explain the different kinds of child abuse and the warning signs that should concern any early years worker.

Chapter 2 explains how the child protection system works as a whole, including the legal framework within which professionals must operate in England and Wales. It is important to understand the broader context so that you can place your own work within this.

The other chapters in the book focus specifically on your own work and how you, as an early years worker, might become involved in the child protection process. Chapter 3 covers how child protection can be established within the systems of your own early years service; Chapters 4 and 5 cover the detail of what you may contribute to the protection of individual children within your early years setting; and Chapter 6 covers how general good practice can make a difference to children's welfare and support their ability to keep themselves safe from harm.

1

Understanding Child Abuse

Child abuse in context

In broad terms, child abuse is:

- Doing something to a child that should not be done: anything that will injure them physically, distress them deeply emotionally or seriously disrupt their natural development.
- Failing to do something for a child that should be done, for the sake of their well-being, safety or continued positive development.

Within this very broad framework there are different types of action, or inaction, that could be considered abusive in their consequences for children, and these are covered in this chapter.

Development of a child protection approach

Moves to establish effective child protection developed in the second half of the twentieth century. Since the 1960s the following developments have taken place.

- The acceptance of the reality of child abuse – the acknowledgement that child abuse happens and that it cannot be explained away as a few isolated incidents.
- A greater awareness of the reality of different types of child abuse.
- A growing acceptance that such ill-treatment is abusive and cannot be excused as falling within the bounds of parental or institutional discipline.
- The growing conviction that no civilised society should tolerate the abuse of its youngest and most vulnerable citizens. So, there have to be limits to family privacy and the right of parents to decide how to treat their children. In a similar way, the heads and staff of institutions should be accountable for how they treat children and young people.
- The accepted approach of listening to children and realising that what they say is as likely to be true as what an adult says. The previous approach was to believe the adult's version in any conflict.

Physical Abuse and Ill-Treatment

Child protection, as we know it now, is a relatively recent development, but it would be a mistake to assume that previous generations were unaware or uncaring about the ill-treatment of children. Even when physical punishment was far more socially acceptable, there was concern that children might be deliberately injured by their parents.

In 1868 Ambroise Tardieu, who was a professor of legal medicine in Paris, described the deaths of children from battering or burning. In the same year, Athol Johnson noted that some children were arriving with repeated bone fractures at the Hospital for Sick Children in London. There was a strong resistance to believing that parents could deliberately and frequently injure their own children; the injuries could also be plausibly explained by the effect of rickets, a condition that weakens the bones and which was very common in children at that time.

The first British Prevention of Cruelty to Children Act was passed in 1889 and created the option of prosecution. Prior to this law, any actions on behalf of children were taken personally by relatives or neighbours. The National Society for the Prevention of Cruelty to Children (NSPCC) was established in 1884 and developed a national network of centres and inspectors. The NSPCC's long tradition of protecting children is the reason that child protection procedures today directly involve this organisation.

Children with repeated, hard to explain, injuries remained a medical puzzle until 1961, when Henry Kempe, in a presentation to the American Academy of Paediatrics, described the **battered child syndrome** and opened up a serious debate claiming that adults, including parents, sometimes intentionally injured children. Tragically it took the non-accidental death of a child to bring the reality of physical abuse effectively into the public arena. In 1973 seven-year-old Maria Colwell was battered to death by her stepfather. Maria was known to be at risk by the local authority and the inquiry in 1974 criticised the lack of communication between the various agencies involved with the family. The child protection register, first known as an 'at risk register', was established in 1975 as a national system to improve contact in such cases between social workers, the police and the medical profession.

Recognition of the physical ill-treatment of children was the first established base of child protection. By the 1980s it had became socially unacceptable to support physical punishment within schools. The Education Act 1986 made corporal punishment illegal in state schools. Independent schools were not obliged to stop the practice, although most do not use this option.

Emotional Abuse and Neglect

There has been a growing understanding that children's development and well-being can be undermined by continuous verbal attacks within the family. Their emotional and physical well-being can also be destroyed by neglect. Although recognised as a real possibility for some children, this kind of abuse is the hardest to prove.

The Existence of Sexual Abuse

Through the 1960s and 1970s there was a growing acknowledgement of the possibility of physical abuse of children by the adults who were supposed to care for their well-being. Through the 1980s another realisation developed: that children might be abused sexually, either within the family (incest) or by other adults trusted to take care of them.

In 1985 the national telephone network, Childline, was established, which offered children and young people a chance to talk in confidence and made a public statement of commitment to child protection from abuse.

The events in Cleveland during 1987 brought sexual abuse into public awareness when 121 children were diagnosed by doctors as having been sexually abused. Most were separated from their parents, although the majority were later returned. Like many high profile cases of sexual abuse, the events of Cleveland are still discussed and there is certainly no agreement about who was in the right.

Institutional Abuse

Initially, the focus for abuse was on ill-treatment in children's own homes, but several cases emerged through the late 1980s and 1990s that showed how professionals could also be involved in systematic abuse. Scandals emerged from children's residential homes, educational and day care settings. Abuse could be physical, sexual or emotional, was sometimes perpetrated by single individuals, and in other cases by more than one member of staff.

A Personal Example

Recognition of sexual abuse has only really developed in the last couple of decades, but it is by no means a new problem for children. Both my parents have described to me incidents from their own childhoods when respected local adults were charged with child molestation and sent to prison.

This occurred in two very different communities during the 1930s: a Welsh mining town and a small Hampshire village. In one case it was the local Scout troop leader and in the other it was the choir master. Neither of my parents experienced direct problems with the people concerned, but they told me how the local children sensed something wrong in the behaviour of each of these men, even when they were not the children being molested.

In the case of the Scout master, boys had complained to their parents that they did not want to go away to camp with this man and his wife, but the children's concerns were usually dismissed. The choir master was known as a 'creep' and none of the girls wished to sit too close to him. In each case, local parents were shocked when the man was eventually arrested and imprisoned; the children were not at all surprised.

COMMENTS

- It would be inappropriate for you to ask anyone about such experiences out of the blue, but you may find that through conversation, reading or television programmes you will extend your understanding of how sexual abuse was part of the experience of some children in previous generations.
- Many children will not have been affected directly, but will have childhood memories of adults whom they sensed were not to be trusted, who overstepped unspoken boundaries in how adults should relate to children.
- A strong theme in teaching children self-protection is to support them by trusting their feelings of unease about any adult and to take them seriously if they express such concerns.

Who are the abusers?

Children are most likely to be abused or neglected by people who are well known to them: adults or young people who are family, friends or in a position of trust and responsibility. The idea that children are at great risk from strangers has arisen from media attention to the very few tragic cases of child abduction or unprovoked physical and/or sexual attack.

The most likely abuser is an adult, but young people (under 18) have been known to abuse children known to them or for whom they are temporarily responsible. Actions between children that are judged physically abusive if carried out by an adult, will probably be dealt with through anti-bullying programmes in schools or early years centres (bullying has been taken with considerably more seriousness over the last decade or so).

The most likely sexual abuser is an adult male, but women do also inflict physical abuse or neglect on children. Sexual abuse by women does happen but is very unusual. Young people and even children have been involved in the sexual abuse of peers or younger children and some vicious bullying has taken on a sexual element. When under-18s are involved in abuse it is very likely that any action would include child protection concerns for the abusing children themselves as well as for those whom they have abused. It is very possible that children who abuse have themselves been on the receiving end of ill-treatment or some kind of abuse.

Patterns of abusive behaviour and likely abusers vary enormously. Abusers come from all social and ethnic groups and no predictions can be made with absolute certainty that a particular individual is very likely or unlikely to abuse. Abusers have included members of professions that are based on trust, such as youth workers, social workers in residential homes, day care and educational staff and clergy.

There are a number of possible reasons why people abuse or neglect children and some of these are discussed within this chapter. Of course, explanations are neither excuses nor justification for allowing abuse to continue unchallenged. But useful work, that will help children, has to take some account of how the abusing situation may have arisen.

How common is child abuse?

One way of assessing the extent of child abuse is to look at the numbers of children on child protection registers. In March 1994 there were 34,900 children on all the registers in England. Of these, 37% had suffered some physical injury, 30% had been neglected, 28% had experienced sexual abuse and 13% had been emotionally abused. These percentages add up to more than 100% because children can be listed under more than one category of abuse. The actual incidence of abuse is higher than the total number of children on the registers because, however hard the social services and related professions work, some cases will never come to light. Additionally, the same children do not appear on the registers every year. For instance, in the year that ended in March 1995, 34,954 children were on registers in England, but during that year the names of 30,225 children had been taken off and 30,444 added.

The relative proportion of boys and girls varies by age and the category of abuse. In the 1994 figures there were slightly more boys in the under-10s and the reverse was true for the over-10s, but this difference was not great. Boys feature more than girls in the physical abuse category but girls are over-represented in the sexual abuse category.

Another way investigators have used to judge the extent of abuse is to ask adults to recall the events of their childhood and to classify bad experiences on whether they would be judged as abusive. This method has been used in trying to survey the extent of sexual abuse, but the approach has problems. For instance, David Finkelhor, an expert in the study of child sexual abuse, reviewed studies of sexual abuse in the United States. He reported that, depending on whose figures you took, you would predict prevalence rates in the general population of anything from 6–62% for females and 3–31% for males. The working definition of sexual abuse varied from minor, though unwanted sexual attentions (which the study respondents themselves might not classify as abuse), to increasingly intrusive forms of physical contact. The percentages were highest when the definition of sexual abuse was made very wide.

Physical abuse

Physical abuse is defined as the actual or likely physical injury to a child. Children may be physically abused through direct attack or by an adult's deliberate failure to protect them from injury or suffering. Physical abuse, with accompanying neglect, is the most common form of maltreatment of children and is the most common cause of death from abuse. It is important to bear this in mind, since some research implies that sexual abuse is the most prevalent form of abuse.

When abused, children may be hit, shoved or shaken hard. It is potentially dangerous to shake any child with violence, but babies can be especially at serious risk from shaking because of their limited physical control of a relatively heavy head. The 'Don't shake the baby' leaflet campaign, organised by the Department of Health in the mid 1990s, was launched to bring the real danger to everyone's attention. Children have been bitten, burned or deliberately scalded, squeezed with violence or half-suffocated. Physical abuse has included deliberate poisoning of children with household substances, and the inappropriate use of alcohol, drugs or prescription medicines. Abuse has also included ill-treatment of children that has frightened them, such as being shut in cupboards or other confined and dark spaces.

Signs that should concern you

The most likely warning signs of the physical abuse of children are injuries, perplexing illnesses, or a continuing pattern of accidents that befall a child for which the responsible adult(s) give no believable explanation.

The relevant carers will often be the child's parents but some children are cared for by relatives or other adults. The same concern should be triggered in early years settings when the child's injuries or unexplained symptoms are arising within the day or session. Cases of child abuse generally arise within the family but there have been instances when child care or education workers have been responsible for the abuse or neglect.

It is important to recall that young children collect a large number of bumps and bruises in the normal course of their play. Physically bold children, with a limited understanding or concern about risks, can have an early childhood full of minor, but understandable injuries. Even very responsible parents, or early years workers, can find that a child has sustained a more serious injury, such as fractured or broken bones, in a well-supervised setting that has been made as safe as possible. So, a consideration of possible physical abuse has to take into account *both* the visible injury to the child *and* the explanation of how this injury was caused.

This section continues with the signs that should concern you and be taken further – through a conversation with the parent and/or discussion with your line manager. The steps you should take will be laid out in your setting's child protection procedures and are discussed in detail in Chapters 3 and 4.

Unexplained Accidents

You should be concerned about children who have injuries for which there is no obvious explanation. Be wary about improbable explanations or excuses given by an adult or by the child, when the explanation keeps changing or if there is a refusal to discuss the reason for an injury. (See page 101 for more about indicators to accidental and non-accidental injury.)

However, initial unlikely explanations from children cannot necessarily be seen as proof of abuse. A child may, for instance, give a strange reason for an injury but further discussion with the child and parent could reveal that the child produced the story because he was covering up for something he should not have been doing. The child is worried about getting into trouble and cannot foresee that his version of events could bring suspicion on his parent.

A continuing pattern of odd accidents, even if each individual explanation seems possible, may be a warning sign of abuse or a neglectful lack of supervision. Again, a worrying pattern cannot be taken as proof without further exploration. A child may be being abused or so poorly supervised that she is hurting herself. But some children have problems of physical co-ordination or failing eyesight. A few children have brittle bone disease which means that very minor accidents can create fractures and breaks. Anyone involved has to keep an open mind when the worries first emerge.

Visible Injuries

Injuries may include bruising, black eyes, fractured or broken limbs, burn or bite marks. Bruises to the bony parts of children's bodies, such as elbows and knees, are more usually the result of normal childhood bumps and scrapes, whereas bruising to the softer parts, such as upper arms, thighs and cheeks, may result from pinching, biting or beating.

Many children have slight differences of coloration in their skin. This variation can look like bruising on dark-skinned children, especially of African-Caribbean, Mediterranean and Asian origin but these are naturally occurring and are known as mongolian blue spots. They have a defined edge and are a consistent slate blue in colour, unlike genuine bruising that tends to vary in shade and changes over a period of days.

Children may sometimes tell you that someone is hurting them, but often they are as concerned about hiding their ill-treatment as the adults who are inflicting it. You should therefore be alert to a child who is very reluctant to undress for games or a routine medical check, or to uncover themselves in hotter weather – *unless* there is an alternative explanation for their unease. Some children will not undress due to cultural or religious reasons and these should be respected. Others are self-conscious about their bodies because other children have been rude about their size, shape or skin problems, such as eczema.

A Child's Behaviour

There may be behavioural signs that all is not well with a child, and the underlying reason may sometimes, but not always, be that there is a pattern of abuse. You should be concerned about children who are very reluctant to go home at the end of the day or session, or resistant to going with a particular family member. Self-destructive tendencies in children are a warning sign of emotional disturbance, although not necessarily abuse. You should not ignore patterns of self-harm, such as pulling out their hair or banging their heads. Children who are persistently aggressive towards other children in the centre need help and you should explore the source of their behavioural problems.

ACTIVITIES and QUESTIONS

The majority of parents whose children sustain minor or more major injuries are *not* abusing their children and it is important to bear this in mind. You will find more on positive ways to communicate with parents in Chapter 5, but use this activity to develop your insight into the parent's perspective when someone is questioning an injury to their child.

Your early years setting should keep an accident book, in which you log any injuries that children experience while they are under your responsibility. Take a considered look at all the incidents over the last month.

1 Do one or two children appear much more often than others?
2 Are there some incidents which gave rise to some surprisingly serious injuries in the children given the situations in which they occurred?
3 Are there some areas of the setting or pieces of equipment that seem to be the focus of more minor accidents than others?

A careful review of the accident book can often point to improvements in practice in an early years setting, or tell you that one or two children seem to be especially vulnerable. But imagine that someone used these incidents to challenge you:

- 'You're clearly not taking proper care of Sam. Otherwise how come he keeps having all these accidents?'
- 'You can't be telling me the whole truth. Erin couldn't have got this badly hurt just playing about on a grassy slope!'

How might you feel, or how have you felt, when put firmly on the spot by a parent who is not satisfied with your explanation of how his/her child was injured in the centre? Discuss these issues with your colleagues and use their insights to help you consider both sides of this kind of difficult conversation.

Possible factors leading to physical abuse

Children are physically abused due to a number of factors. It is important to understand the possible factors because work with families and individuals has to take account of circumstances, but these are not, of course, excuses or justifications for abusing children.

- Family stresses are sometimes taken out on child(ren). Financial and other worries may make parents less patient or they may focus their anger on a person close at hand, such as a child.
- Young parents or carers who are unsupported may become overwhelmed with the responsibility of looking after babies or young children. Their frustration or panic may combine with a genuine ignorance of how their actions can be harmful or neglectful to children.
- Physical discipline may get seriously out of hand as a parent's frustration or temper leads to fiercer attempts to control a child's perceived misbehaviour.
- Some adults, as a result of their own experiences, relish inflicting cruelty on others, and children are an easy target. Powerless adults may enjoy wielding a sense of power over the young and vulnerable.
- Within families, one child may be abused, whilst another is left unharmed. The abuser(s) might unreasonably perceive that this child is the bad one or the unwanted child.
- The abuse of children may be part of a broader pattern of domestic violence in a home.
- A small minority of adults who deliberately injure children are seeking attention for themselves through the apparent medical emergencies in

their children. This pattern is called Munchausen Syndrome by proxy – see below.

Risks from domestic violence

The term **domestic violence** is generally used to mean male violence towards their female partners or ex-partners. Statistics indicate that men are most often the perpetrators of violence in the home, but it has to be recognised that in a small minority of cases it is the woman who is violent towards her partner and/or their children. Domestic violence is not only linked with poverty and/or stressful living conditions; the situation can arise in any social class or ethnic group.

Children are adversely affected by living in a home where there are regular violent disputes. Their emotional well-being and psychological development is poorly affected even if they do not suffer any physical abuse themselves. The likely risks are that:

- Children become distressed by continuing arguments in their home and by the threat of possible violence. They may be torn by conflicting loyalties between their parents and can also be pulled into the damaging secret that nobody outside the family is to know how bad matters have become.
- Children may fail to be protected in a home full of violence. Conflicts between the adults may erupt into physical attack and the children can be caught in the middle. The adults may not intend to injure the children and do not directly attack them, but their violent behaviour could injure the children nevertheless.
- Men prone to violence might also attack children or threaten to do so in order to control their partners. Children in violent homes are sometimes physically or sexually abused by the father or stepfather.
- Women under extreme stress are not in a position to offer their children the kind of support that is necessary for healthy development and some mothers divert their frustration and anger onto the children. Children in their turn may become aggressive to other children, or may turn in on themselves to become distressed and withdrawn.

Munchausen Syndrome by proxy

Munchausen Syndrome was first described in 1951 by psychiatrist Richard Asher who was seeing adult patients who deliberately made themselves ill, or claimed to have a variety of serious symptoms, in order to gain medical attention. These people often sought very intrusive medical procedures, such as unnecessary operations, at a number of different hospitals. (The name of the syndrome actually comes from the highly unlikely tales told by Baron von Munchausen, a traveller and writer.)

In 1977 the term was extended by Professor Roy Meadow to describe the behaviour of adults who claimed that a child in their care was seriously ill when this was not the case. Adult carers, in most cases the mother, reported a series of imaginary symptoms for the child or interfered with medical investigations to make the claims appear supported. In a few cases adults were actually causing injury to the child which led to dramatic symptoms. Meadow called this pattern of disturbed adult behaviour **Munchausen Syndrome by proxy**, and it has also been known as **Meadow's Syndrome**. This situation is specifically included as a form of physical abuse of children.

It is important to realise that this syndrome is rare, and so one should not assume that this is a likely explanation when a parent is persistently concerned about the health of a child and there is no easy or immediate explanation of what is the matter. There is plenty of anecdotal evidence to show that concerned parents have been proved right in their worries, although professionals could not initially find a diagnosis.

Parents and other carers who claim healthy children are ill, or who deliberately harm children to create a medical emergency, seem to feed off the drama of the situation. They seek the reflected attention onto themselves of having a dramatically or frequently ill child. Some seem to like the kudos of being seen as an important and self-sacrificing carer for the child. The end result for children is unnecessary illness and medical intervention, and confusion over their own health and well-being.

Female circumcision

In the 1996 revision of *Working Together* (guidance for agencies and professionals directly involved in child protection), the Department of Health specifically included female circumcision as a form of physical abuse. Female circumcision, in any of its forms, has been illegal in Britain since the Abolition of Female Circumcision Act of 1985. The recognition that this practice is a form of abuse has led to the phrase, **female genital mutilation**.

Female circumcision is practised by some Muslim and Christian communities in North African countries such as Somalia and the Sudan and Middle Eastern countries such as the Yemen. Muslims and Christians who reject the practice argue that there is no basis in either the Qur'an or the Bible for what is a cultural and not a religious tradition. Communities and families who promote female circumcision regard it as a crucial part of how girls become women and a means to ensure that daughters are marriageable. Families living in the UK have been able to find some doctors who are prepared to circumcise their daughters and some traditional circumcisers operate in this country. Otherwise, mothers or grandmothers take the girls back to the family's country of origin in order to obtain the operation.

The practice has been made illegal in Britain because the procedure results in considerably greater mutilation of the genital area of females than the usual circumcision procedure for males. The circumcision itself can be very painful since traditional circumcisers do not necessarily use pain relief. Girls can bleed dangerously and be left with pelvic infections, gynaecological problems and later difficulties with childbirth.

The issue of female circumcision is one in which child protection concerns are in inevitable conflict with the wish to respect the usual practices of some religious or cultural groups. It is an important reminder that respect for any cultural practices should never override concern for children's well-being. The most important guiding principle is that a cultural practice should not lead to the injury or ill-treatment of a child. Child protection teams who face this issue have to be ready to justify their stance from the legal perspective and in terms of the well-being of the girls involved. Teams also need to offer support for those families and girls who wish to break with tradition, since they are likely to face hostility from their community. As an early years worker, you are unlikely to encounter the practice unless you work in a school or after-school club, since girls from these communities tend to be circumcised at around seven to eight years of age.

There is not an equivalent stance about male circumcision, although many people feel that this is an inappropriate practice unless there are very clear medical indications in favour of the removal of a boy's foreskin. In previous generations the circumcision of baby boys was more common in England on the grounds of easier personal hygiene, but this has now been discredited. Some Jewish and Muslim groups regard male circumcision as an important religious and cultural rite.

Children who are HIV-positive

In their booklet, *Children and HIV – guidance for local authorities* (1992, revised version due in 1998) the Department of Health made it clear that the fact that a child is HIV-positive is *not* in itself sufficient reason to place the child on the child protection register. Services should be provided for children on the same basis as their peers.

Certainly, some families whose children are HIV-positive may be afraid to seek help because of their wariness of local child protection procedures. The way in which a child has become infected might, on the other hand, give rise to child protection issues, for instance, if there was evidence that the HIV infection had been transmitted through sexual abuse, or through gross neglect of the child leading to contact with infected syringe needles.

Early years workers will not necessarily know if a child is HIV-positive, since it is not required that carers are informed. Normal good practice for hygiene and first aid in the centre should provide adequate protection.

Neglect

Neglect is the failure to care properly for a child. It can be difficult to assess in practice and it has received a lot less attention from the media than other types of child abuse. All of the following are examples of neglect:

- Inadequate food so that children are malnourished or actually starving.
- Inadequate clothing for the time of year so that children are cold and ill throughout the winter months. Children may also be made to sleep in unheated bedrooms with insufficient bedclothes for the temperature.
- Neglect of children's basic physical needs so that they are dirty, remain for ages in unchanged nappies or have infections that would have improved with basic medical attention.
- Leaving young children home alone.

It is important not to underestimate the risks of severe neglect to babies and children. Some children have died as the direct consequence of neglect, and others have been in a very poor state of health and general development when the seriousness of their situation has been realised.

Various inquiries into child abuse have revealed that some families who neglect their children do so for a long time, perhaps years, even with social work support, without anybody realising that the family has gone beyond the bounds of 'acceptable parenting'. The input of an early years centre can be crucial in this kind of situation because workers can observe and record the consequences for the child. The Department of Health guidelines for the practice of social workers, *Protecting children: a guide for social workers undertaking a comprehensive assessment*, (also known as 'The Orange Book' so called because of the colour of its cover) stresses that, 'The neglected child requires the same structured and rigorous approach to assessment and treatment as any other abused child.' A concern that parents are doing what appears to be their best under difficult circumstances has to be balanced by an objective view of what is happening to the children.

Signs that should concern you

Children who are neglected might show one or more of the following symptoms of their poor care:

- They may be thin (health records show that they fail to put on weight). A malnourished child can be tired and lethargic.
- If you feed children in your setting, you may find that a child arrives desperate for food and eats a large amount when it is available. Their hunger may be noticeably greater after the weekend.
- Children may be regularly dressed inappropriately for the weather, for instance, thin summer clothes and sandals on a cold winter day. They may show signs of being cold on a regular basis, for instance, chapped hands, chilblains or unnaturally reddened skin in a white child.
- Children and their clothes may be dirty and/or smelly. Soiled clothes, such as underwear, may be put back on a child rather than removed for washing.
- Parents may be unreliable in bringing the child to the setting on a regular basis or in picking the child up at the end of the day or session. The parents themselves may be in an unsafe state to care for children: drunk or showing the effects of drugs.
- Children may have untreated medical conditions or infections that are left to worsen rather than improved with basic home care or by seeking medical treatment.
- Sometimes all the children within a family are neglected, but it is possible that one child will be singled out and visibly treated worse than the other children.

Children who are neglected sometimes fall into the group described as showing a **failure to thrive.** However, babies and children should not be classified as failing to thrive unless there has been careful assessment over a period of time and the experience and records of all the professionals involved with the child and the family have been taken into consideration. Failure to thrive cannot be diagnosed just by plotting a baby or child on average growth charts; these charts are based on variations around the average and some babies and children will always be on the 'light' side, just as some are on the 'heavy' side. Height and weight has a genetic component and small parents are likely to produce children who are smaller and lighter than the average. Some babies and children have digestion or allergy problems which affect their ability to keep food down or to digest it properly. Other children have eating problems and parents' understandable concern over mealtimes may inadvertently worsen the difficulties. Such families may appreciate advice from early years workers but they are not neglecting their children.

So, a number of possibilities has to be explored when concerns are raised about a child. Records of a child's physical and general development can be crucial in discovering whether a child is being neglected. For instance, a neglected child may be in considerably better health and energy after spending time away from his/her family.

Possible factors leading to neglect

By definition, neglect occurs in families that are functioning poorly but there may be different factors which lead to the difficulties. The distinction is made between **primary parental incompetence**, when parents have very little idea of how to take care of a child, and **secondary parental incompetence**, when circumstances are weighing down a parent who would otherwise be able to manage. Neither situation can be allowed to continue at the cost of the child's well-being, but some understanding of what is going wrong, and why, is important for decisions about how best to help.

In the case of primary parental incompetence, neglect may arise from parents' lack of basic knowledge or understanding, for instance:

- Some parents may not know what to do because their own childhood has given no useful experience of how adults care for children. They may themselves have been abused or neglected as children and have no positive model to help them.
- Parents with severe learning disabilities may not understand what a baby or young child needs and the consequences of poor care.
- Teenage parents who are still very young and without family support may also have little idea of what baby and child care involves. They may

feel overwhelmed by the responsibilities and the change brought about in their lives. Young mothers may also be stunned that a baby whom they hoped would satisfy their own emotional needs is him/herself a very needy individual.

These are all possibilities but, of course, there is no absolute link between these circumstances and child neglect, or abuse. Some adults who have experienced very unhappy or disrupted childhoods are able to be good parents to their own children. They have looked for positive models outside their own childhood or been guided by a supportive partner whose childhood was much happier. Parents with learning disabilities or very young mothers can often cope with appropriate support.

In the case of secondary parental incompetence, families would normally cope under favourable circumstances but adverse events overwhelm the ability of one or both parents to cope and the well-being of the children suffers. For instance:

- Parents may be experiencing extreme financial hardship, debts and all the worries that come in their wake. It is important to realise, however, that some families with serious money worries do not neglect their children. And some families with no financial problems do neglect one or more of their children.
- Physical or mental illness in the family may have incapacitated the main carer of the children. Psychological disturbance in the main carer may also lead him/her deliberately to neglect one child who is seen as a problem, unwanted, or the 'wrong' sex. Alternatively the parent's energy may be diverted to caring for a very sick or elderly family member. The children are being overlooked, effectively forgotten or are unrealistically expected to take care of themselves.
- Parents who have continuing problems of alcoholism, substance abuse and other addictions, like gambling, are likely to lose sight of the needs of their children. Time, attention and family money may be diverted away from the children's needs and towards the addiction.
- In some families deeply held religious or philosophical views may lead to what is judged to be neglect from outside the family. Parents may refuse conventional medicines even when their preferred alternative methods are failing to help a very sick child. Parents may also refuse life-giving interventions such as blood transfusions; Jehovah's Witnesses are opposed to this treatment. These situations are very difficult since, when the consequences may be ruined health or death for the child, an outside authority has to judge the limits to any parent's right to decide.

Emotional abuse

All children who are abused are affected emotionally, to a greater or lesser extent. It is therefore reasonable to say that emotional abuse plays a part in all types of abuse, as all abuse will affect children's sense of security or trust, their belief in themselves as worthwhile individuals who deserve care and their likely feelings in the future towards other children and adults. However, for some children, a pattern of emotional abuse is the main or only form of abuse in their lives.

Emotional abuse is a persistent pattern of deliberate uncaring or emotionally cruel treatment of a child. It can be hard to detect and it is important neither to overreact nor to underestimate what appears to be happening to the child. A judgement of emotional abuse has to take account of patterns and the continuing experience of a child or children in a family or in a setting such as day care or a school in which the child is regularly targeted for emotional abuse. Persistent or severe emotional ill-treatment or rejection of a child has a negative effect on their all-round development and behaviour. Children need to experience affection, security and encouragement and if these experiences are denied to them, they can doubt their own worth, their ability to make relationships or their capacity to learn and deal with life. Children may be physically unharmed but so badly affected by emotional abuse that they are in poor health or react by harming themselves.

Emotional abuse might take the following forms:

- Children may be verbally abused, told for example that they are 'stupid', 'useless', 'ugly' or 'should never have been born'.
- They may be subjected to continuous criticism or faced with unrealistically high adult expectations, which no child could ever meet.
- Their interests and achievements may be ridiculed or compared unfavourably with someone else, perhaps a favoured sibling.
- Any apparent affection felt by the parents is made dependent on the child's behaviour or achievements. The child never feels sure of his/her parents' love nor can easily predict what will make them withdraw their affection.
- Children may be overprotected to an unrealistic extent so that they cannot gain any sense of confidence or appropriate self-reliance. The continuous message is that they are incompetent or unable to deal with circumstances outside the home.

- Communication with the child may be distorted so that the adult uses his/her maturity inappropriately to make the child feel guilty for family situations that are not and cannot be the child's responsibility.
- Children may also be emotionally damaged by experiences of domestic violence (see page 11) or family conflict. Children may feel torn between two disputing parents and the adults may deliberately use the children to vent their own feelings or to attack their partner verbally.

Signs that should concern you

No adult, however caring, manages to be patient and considerate with children all the time. Parents are not perfect and sometimes they get cross or their own concerns temporarily overwhelm them. In an early years setting, workers may look back and feel that they did not give a child the attention s/he needed or that they jumped to an unfair conclusion over the behaviour of another child. But adults such as these, who treat children well and with respect, will admit their mistakes and make the effort to put right their oversights. They will listen to another adult, fellow-parent or colleague who points out that a child is being treated too severely or that their expectations of the child are unrealistic. An adult who is emotionally abusing a child carries on with this treatment regardless of the obvious distress of the child.

Families can go through difficult times and parents try their utmost not to take out their stress on their children. Some parents respond well to help from relatives, friends or trusted early years workers. They acknowledge the difficult situation that has developed and are prepared to work towards changing it. Other parents, and some carers, are resistant to acknowledge what is happening or to change the situation. They persist in believing that the child deserves the emotional abuse.

Any of the following patterns of behaviour in children should concern you, although none of these alone is proof of emotional abuse.

- When your observations and records show that a child is developmentally delayed – especially if your usual efforts to help a child are not making much progress.
- When children indicate, through words and body language, that they think they are worthless, stupid or unattractive.
- When children persistently blame themselves or seem to expect you to blame them or punish them. Be aware of children who are very distressed by their mistakes (though some are by temperament, as well as experience, hard on themselves, or set themselves tough standards, so you cannot afford to jump to conclusions).

- When children harm themselves with persistent hair pulling, picking at their skin or head banging, or have compulsive rituals such as very regular and lengthy hand washing.
- When children find it difficult to make friends and the reason seems to be that they do not see themselves as worthy of being liked.
- When children are either mistrusting of adults and appear to expect them to be unpredictable and unpleasant, or are prone to cling in an undiscriminating way to any adult who is kind to them.

Possible factors leading to emotional abuse

There are different factors that cause adults to abuse children emotionally:

- Some adults may be reliving their own childhood experiences of cruel words and relentless criticism. It may not occur to them that there are better ways to treat children, or they may really believe that they are unaffected by the treatment they received, and so they cannot possibly be harming their child(ren).
- Adults' own troubles may be projected onto children. In a life plagued by worries and doubts about their own competence, some adults relieve their own stress by bullying and abusing children. Sometimes parents explicitly blame one or more of their children for causing their problems or 'ruining my life by being born!'
- Some emotional abuse seems to arise from an adult's dislike of a child. The abuse is excused on the grounds that the child is persistently naughty, awkward or insolent. In group situations, adults who abuse one child can sometimes seem to be motivated by the expectation that picking on this child will keep the rest of the group in line.
- Emotional cruelty by adults may arise through an abuse of their authority: the adult feels powerful by ridiculing a child or always finding something to criticise.
- Some adults believe that children will not learn without being hit, or the threat of such punishment. In a similar way, other adults believe children will only learn by being criticised and that encouraging words will only make them proud and bigheaded.

Sexual abuse

Sexual abuse is defined as the actual or likely sexual exploitation of a child or adolescent who is dependent or developmentally immature (because of age in years or the impact of learning disabilities). The point about sexual abuse is that the younger, more dependent or vulnerable individual is not in the position to give consent to acts that would be acceptable between genuinely consenting adults. Some sexual abuse involves acts of force that would constitute a crime even if adults were the only people involved.

Sexual abuse of children may involve full sexual intercourse, but abusive use of children in a sexual way also includes sexual fondling, masturbation, oral or anal sex or attempts to involve children in these acts, and involving children in sexual exhibitionism. It is also regarded as abusive to coerce children into looking at pornographic photographs or films or to make them take part in such filming. Statistics indicate that more girls than boys have experienced some form of sexual abuse, although both are at risk. Some children are abused only once, or for a very short period of time, but for some children the experience continues for years.

Signs that should concern you

As with any kind of child abuse, there is no list of definite signs of sexual abuse. Any of the following observations should concern you but are not in themselves absolute evidence of sexual abuse.

Within normal development children are highly physical in their contact with one another and often like to be close to adults whom they trust and like. They show curiosity about their own and others' bodies and are relatively uninhibited in their behaviour, although this is the case in some more than others. Any concerns must be placed within an understanding of the normal range of children's development and their current grasp of socially accepted behaviour in private and public.

THE CHILD'S BEHAVIOUR

- Highly sexual behaviour from young children, rather than affectionate physical contact, should concern you. It is not within normal development for children to persist in trying to make physically intimate contact with other children or with adults, especially once another child or adult has said 'No'.
- Children who are being abused may express their worries and experiences in their play with dolls or small figures. They may also produce sexually explicit paintings or drawings. Any sense you make of the concern must allow for the fact that many young children are interested in bottoms and 'willies', so you must consider how far this child's play is out of the ordinary.

- Young children often fiddle with their private parts but you should be concerned if a child seems to be masturbating on a regular basis.
- What children say may concern you if it shows a sexual knowledge or curiosity unlikely for their age. Again, it is important to have a broad framework in which to make sense of any concern. Some parents are honest in answering children's questions and so a four- or five-year-old may be interested and well-informed about 'where babies come from'.
- Sometimes distressed children will tell you about unhappy secrets or games about which they are uneasy. When children disclose sexual, or any other, abuse it is important to continue the conversation with care (see page 86).
- Some abused children react to their experience by regressing in development, for instance, in their toilet training, or by having nightmares and daytime fears. A formerly calm child may become unexpectedly aggressive or a confident child very withdrawn.
- You should never ignore any form of self-harm from children or talk that suggests they feel they are unworthy or that life is not worth living. This kind of behaviour is not just a phase and should be addressed, but remember that you cannot be sure that abuse is the cause.
- Children do not like everyone equally and sometimes they dislike or are uncomfortable with someone for reasons that have nothing to do with abuse. However, you should wonder if a child is very definite about not wanting to be taken home by a particular person or talks about not liking a particular baby-sitter. You cannot jump to conclusions but it is appropriate to discuss these issues with the child's parent(s). It is essential to follow up any indications that a child might seem very wary about being in the charge of a particular member of staff or the arrival of a frequent visitor to the centre.

Physical Conditions

Some physical symptoms in children should concern you. Again, none of these are absolute evidence of abuse, and could be attributed to another physical condition that needs attention.

- Pain, itching or redness in the genital or anal area needs medical attention but the condition could be the result of thrush or threadworms. Both of these cause very uncomfortable itching and can lead to broken skin if the child has scratched vigorously. Persistent constipation can cause redness and anal fissures or bleeding from the strain.

- Bruising or bleeding in the genital or anal area again needs medical attention, as does any child's clear discomfort in walking or sitting down. But you have to keep an open mind, as does the doctor who examines the child, because children do sometimes slip or fall and land heavily on their crotch area.
- A vaginal discharge or apparent infection in a girl should be checked. Again, be aware that children sometimes stick small objects into their bodily orifices and are then unable to retrieve them. An otherwise harmless object can create an infection if left. However, if a medical examination of a child revealed a sexually transmitted disease, it would be reasonable for the doctor to suspect that the child had been abused.

In an early years setting, concerns should be expressed to a line manager and discussed with the parent(s), but a thorough investigation would be needed to establish if the child was being sexually abused. Medical examinations are sometimes part of an inquiry into sexual abuse but, contrary to what many people believe, a medical examination only rarely produces evidence that points directly to sexual abuse.

Abusers and possible factors leading to sexual abuse

CHILD MOLESTERS AND PAEDOPHILES

Study of sexual abusers has shown that a child molester behaves differently from a paedophile.

- A **child molester** may target children and young people because they are available or easier to intimidate. This person may have had adult sexual relationships or be in such a relationship at the same time as abusing a child. What seems to happen is that such people turn to children when they feel under stress or rejected in their adult relationship. They find children – their own, stepchildren or children of friends – less threatening and justify their abuse on the grounds that they are not harming the child or the child sought and accepted this form of affection from them. A child molester, if not stopped, may continue the sexual relationship with the child as s/he grows into adulthood.
- A **paedophile** is someone who is sexually attracted specifically to children and young people below the age of sexual consent. Children are a paedophile's preferred object of sexual activity and fantasy. Paedophiles may spend time gaining a position of trust with children, in a job or voluntary activity. Some target particular children and spend time getting to know the child and gaining the trust of their family – a

process called 'grooming'. Paedophiles lose sexual interest in children as they grow out of childhood toward adulthood. Paedophiles may be attracted to child pornography and in some cases this activity is part of their system of abuse.

Some sexual abusers have themselves been abused as children and have a distorted understanding of how to form affectionate relationships. They may be exercising power over children because they feel incompetent in relations with adults. However, by no means all children who have been abused go on to abuse others.

Under the Sex Offenders Act 1997 convicted sex offenders (or those cautioned about such an offence) have to register with the local police. Guidelines from the Act make it likely that the police will inform the heads and managers of local schools, nurseries or preschools when a known paedophile is living in the area. However, this information has to be kept confidential, so at the time of writing it is hard to see how it could be used to protect children. Clearer guidance may emerge in due course.

YOUNG ABUSERS

Sometimes children or young people who are being sexually abused start to abuse others while they are themselves still young. The inappropriate or abusive behaviour of a child may be the first warning sign that they are, or have been, sexually abused. The NCH Action for Children project has identified three main reasons why children might start to abuse:

- An adult abuser may coerce one child or young person into inflicting abuse on others.
- An abused child who has become very sexual in his or her behaviour may seek sexual encounters with peers because this is the only way s/he has learned to make close contact.
- An abused child who has been made to feel powerless may act in a sexual way towards a younger or weaker child in order to feel powerful him/herself.

ORGANISED GROUPS

The majority of sexual abusers act individually. However, there have been some cases of groups of adults engaging in systematic sexual abuse of children. Such cases are rare but those that have been exposed show the following patterns:

- Systematic sexual or physical abuse has become established in professional settings such as day care centres or residential children's homes. Children are coerced into secrecy or told, with tragic justification in some children's homes' scandals, that nobody will believe them if they tell because they are bad children with a track record of misbehaviour and absconding.
- Rare instances of systematic abuse in families have involved either several generations in the same family or a linked group of local families. Organised abuse in such cases has involved men, women, boys and girls, although there are still more men involved than women.
- Organised paedophile rings have been uncovered. Such networks more usually involve men who abuse boys, although women and girls have sometimes been involved. Such rings pass children between adults and are often linked with child pornography.

The activities of some of the established cases of groups abusing children have given rise to claims of satanic sexual abuse. The claims of some writers in America are extraordinary and ignore all normal rules of evidence. Considered research in America and in Britain does not support the claims of extensive satanic abuse in either society. However, some of the groups who abuse use bizarre rituals and props to intimidate and silence children. These activities do not seem to have been genuine satanic activities, but the children have believed that the adults had strange powers over them. Groups of abusers have also used systematic cruelty and ill-treatment of children (such as shutting children in cupboards for long periods of time) in order to disorientate them and make them more compliant, through fear, to tolerate perverted sexual practices.

The harm of sexual abuse

Unless the sexual practices are intrusive or particularly violent, children are less likely to suffer physical injury than to be psychologically damaged by the experience. Sexual abuse can have a tremendous short- and longer-term impact on children and young people:

- It is the responsibility of adults, especially those in positions of trust and in close relationships with children, to help children and young people to establish the boundaries of appropriate physical contact and respect for others. Sexual abusers cross and disrupt the very boundaries that they should be helping to create.
- Sexual abusers confuse and distort children's growing understanding of relationships because they have replaced proper affection with sexual contact. The emotional upheaval, especially within the atmosphere of

coercion and secrecy, disrupts children's legitimate wish for attention and care because these needs are met with an inappropriate sexual reaction.

- Children can experience, and be left with, painful feelings of guilt that somehow they brought the abuse on themselves, or are to blame because they accepted gifts or treats from the abuser. Children's natural wish for physical contact, cuddling and affection is manipulated through sexual abuse and children can be made to feel responsible. Yet it is entirely the adult's responsibility to offer appropriate intimacy to a child or young person.
- When children's disclosures of sexual abuse lead to the break-up of their family, they may feel, or be made to feel by some members of the family, that this crisis is their fault. Children may not be believed or may be made to feel at least partly responsible when the abuser is a respected member of the community and 'not the kind of person who would do this'.
- Depending on the reactions they experience when the abuse is disclosed, children may feel dirty, as if they are unpleasant and unworthy. Abusers may also threaten that they will be disliked and rejected if they break the secret.
- Children should be able to trust adults to protect them and not to violate them. The experience of sexual abuse can leave children feeling powerless and betrayed. The abuse can cause them to mistrust adults in general.
- Children's emotional and sexual development can be disrupted. They may have later doubts about their sexuality and how healthy relationships should operate. Adults who experienced sexual abuse may fear, with some justification, that their later adult partners will be disturbed or reject them if they know what happened to them. Boys abused by men can sometimes experience confusion about their sexual identity; for instance, a boy whose orientation would be heterosexual might wonder if he is homosexual.

Adults, or young people, who sexually abuse children are using those children to satisfy their own sexual desires and impulses. Abusers often claim that the younger, or less mature, individual was a willing partner. However, abusers twist the idea of informed consent. Genuine consent means an agreement within an equal relationship and abusing relationships are unequal. Abusers are in a greater position of power because they are older, larger and/or stronger and may have a position of authority or trust over the child. Abusers often build a web of coercion to try to prevent discovery and reduce the likelihood that a child will be believed. They force children to co-operate and keep the secret since they know they are breaking an important social taboo.

A child's compliance and silence about the sexual abuse may be coerced through various means by the adult or young person who abuses:

- Abusers may threaten to hurt the child or someone they care about.
- Abusers may claim that nobody will believe the child if they tell or that others will blame and despise the child if the abuse is revealed. This threat can be especially effective if the abusing adult is in a position of authority over the child (through family or a professional position) or is a respected member of the local community.
- Some abusers attempt to bribe children with presents or treats and then induce a sense of guilt because the child accepted the gifts or outings.
- Some abusers work to convince children that what they are doing is a normal and acceptable activity within the family or between people who supposedly care for each other.

The abuse of disabled children

Children of any age, sex or ethnic group may be abused, in any of the ways described within this chapter. Additional issues arise over the potential abuse of disabled children and young people.

Children with physical or learning disabilities can be more vulnerable to abuse for a number of reasons, not all of which apply, of course, to every child.

- Children may need more personal physical care because of physical disabilities or they may need help at an older age because of severe learning disabilities. Such care can, of course, be offered with respect and consideration, but disabled children may be vulnerable to anything from poor standards in their care to an abuse of their need for help.
- Unsupported and exhausted parents, or other carers, may snap under the relentless pressure of a very high demand for care.
- Continued intrusive medical procedures necessary for some children's conditions may leave them with an underdeveloped sense of their own privacy or bodily dignity. Abusive behaviour by adults or young people may therefore not seem so unusual or unacceptable.

- Children may have a relatively high number of carers because of their condition or because they attend a number of different specialist facilities. Children may learn that intrusive attention by relative strangers is normal. There may also be no key adult who is keeping a close eye on the child's overall care.
- Children and young people with learning and/or communication disabilities may have difficulty in telling a trusted parent or carer that something wrong is happening to them.
- A high level of physical disability may make it hard for a child to resist an abuser.
- Adults may overlook the need to talk to disabled children and young people about appropriate physical touch and sexuality. The mistaken assumption may be that children are within a protected environment, or that sexual awareness and behaviour is irrelevant to disabled young people.
- Carers may feel (inappropriately) that abuse or maltreatment matters less when it involves disabled children.

Good practice with all children is to offer respectful and appropriate physical care (see page 148) and this is especially important for this vulnerable group:

- Children should be asked about their preferences for their personal care and adults should listen however these wishes are expressed.
- Children should be enabled to partake in their own care as much as possible and receive the adult time and attention they need to do this. Children should also have adult support as they learn, even if the learning is very slow.
- Care routines should not be rushed and children should be treated as individuals so they develop a sense of appropriate respectful treatment. They should know the people who care for them so that they do not start to believe that anyone might appear and deal with their intimate needs.
- Staff groups, in partnership with children's parents, need to discuss ways of working to provide consistency and good practice and for ensuring that disabled children are not vulnerable to abuse.

The consequences of abuse

- Some children are injured or die as a result of physical abuse or severe and persistent neglect. For some, their health and development may be seriously endangered.

- Children who are abused have also experienced a vital breakdown of trust. Often it is the very adults who should be caring for and protecting them that are abusing them.
- Children who have been abused may be left with doubts about themselves as individuals worthy of affection and care. The extent to which this is the case will also depend on how far other responsible adults have been able to help a child who has been abused.
- Children may be distressed, emotionally confused about what has happened and frightened or wary of the future. They may doubt their own ability to take care of themselves or that of trusted adults to protect them.
- There is a risk of setting off a cycle of continued abuse. Some abused children react by abusing others in turn, through anger and distress, as the result of coercion by the abusing adult or in emotional confusion over how you should conduct relationships and handle either affection or conflict.

Caring adults who work with abused children can help them, and support the non-abusing parents of abused children, in ways that will enable children or young people to deal with their experience. You cannot make the experience not have happened but you can make a difference to children in rebuilding their lives and trust in others. Most children who have been abused do not go on to abuse (physically, sexually or emotionally) as adults, or parents themselves. It is estimated that about 30% of abused children become abusers in their turn, so a continuing cycle is a risk but is definitely not inevitable. Although they may bear the emotional scars, many adults who experienced childhood abuse are very clear that they will never behave, or allow anyone else to behave, in that way to their children.

Case studies

A number of short case studies now follow. These examples are for you to consider, and ideally to discuss with colleagues or in your student group with a supervisor.

For each of the case studies, consider the following questions:

- Should this situation concern you? If so, in what way does it concern you?
- Given what you have read in this chapter, do you think that the child in this situation could be experiencing abuse? If so, what type(s) of abuse?

Please note that you might be still be concerned, but not feel that the situation was abusive as such.

You might return to one or more of these case studies when you have read more of the book, especially Chapters 3 and 4. At that point you could consider the following questions:

- **Should you talk with the parent in this situation? What will you say? Practise some real phrases, or explore the situation in a role play with a colleague or fellow-student.**
- **What further information might you, or your senior worker, seek?**

Clement

You work in a local authority children's centre. Clement, who is two years old, has started at your centre this week. Clement seems happy and communicates with single words and a few two-word phrases, but he has very little idea of what to do with the play materials that you would usually give to his age group and is keener to handle the baby toys. He cannot walk but stands steadily holding onto a firm surface and moves along by hand holds.

The health visitor has told you that Clement was found a place in the centre because she realised that the boy's mother and grandmother did not let him out of his cot. They both expressed great worries about the potential dangers to Clement if they let him roam around their flat, or if they took him out into the local neighbourhood. Both women seem caring towards Clement but the settling-in time at the centre has been hard, as his grandmother has been especially concerned about Clement's safety in the playroom and the centre garden.

Heather

You have recently joined the staff of a small private nursery school. Heather is nearly four years old and has been attending the school for six months. She is an articulate girl and has started to talk to you about what she has done at the weekend or the previous evening. In a conversation with you yesterday, Heather was describing a film she had watched on television that you know did not start until 11 pm. You said to her, 'You were up very late, Heather. Did Mummy know you were watching that film?' Heather replied, 'Oh, Mummy was with John. They were in the bedroom, doing . . . well, you know what.'

Today you notice that Heather is playing with Jack in the home corner. When you look more closely you realise that Heather is sitting astride Jack and bouncing up and down. She is making grunting noises that sound very like orgasm. At that moment a colleague goes into the home corner and pulls Heather off Jack, saying, 'None of that, Heather. Don't be silly.' In a coffee break later, the other member of staff explains, 'I should have told you, we have to watch Heather. She tries that sort of stuff with the little boys. Poor kid, it's not her fault – goodness knows what she sees at home, but we can't have it here.'

DANNY

Danny is the youngest of five boys in the Sanders family. He attends the nursery class where you work and three of the other boys are in the primary school. Danny is frequently dressed in clothes that are torn, dirty and smelly. His shoes and socks appear to be too small for him and are affecting how he walks. You have spoken with teachers in the classes of the other Sanders boys, who say that these children are usually in clean clothes and sometimes in trainers or sweatshirts that are fashionable. When you mentioned Danny's shoes to his mother, Mrs Sanders told you firmly that she does not have money to burn and Danny should be grateful that he has a choice of clothes that his brothers have not ruined.

You continue to be concerned about Danny. Something he says to you makes you suspicious that he is shut in the cellar but, when asked, Mrs Sanders says that Danny was shut in by one of his brothers as a joke and then the boy forgot. A singed area of hair and what looks like a burn on Danny's scalp is explained as, 'I got the hair dryer a bit close to him last night. Kid wouldn't sit still!'

One afternoon you overhear Mrs Sanders talking to another mother, who is expecting her second child and says she is hoping for a girl this time. Mrs Sanders says that Danny should have been a girl. 'I wanted a daughter. Do you think I wanted all these boys! But Danny fixed that for me. It ruined my insides having him and he was such a sickly little baby. They had to change all his blood when he was born, so it's not like he's really mine, anyway.'

Janice

Janice is three years old and has attended the preschool for several months. She started when her mother had not long given birth to a baby boy, Sachin. Janice's brother is very unwell and has been in hospital several times, but as yet with no definite diagnosis of what is wrong. Her mother is distraught over Sachin's illness and has told you that she is getting very little sleep, what with Sachin screaming and Janice wanting to get into bed with her and her husband.

When she started preschool, Janice was a relatively quiet child but made friends and joined in the play activities, but over the last few weeks you have noticed a significant change in her. She spends a lot of time rocking and hugging herself. She has complained to you of stomach aches and one day says that her bottom is 'so sore'. You tried to speak to Mrs Matthews but she rushed off. The next morning Janice comes to preschool with a long scratch mark over one cheek. Her mother asks to speak with you in private and as soon as you are alone together, she bursts into tears.

Janice's mother admits that she hit her daughter the previous afternoon. She had found Janice trying to put Sachin in the dustbin. 'I just snapped. I hit out at her and my ring scratched her cheek. It's terrible. I said I would never, ever hit one of my children. My father used to hit us; I can't believe I did it.' You take the opportunity to ask about Janice's remark about having a sore bottom. Mrs Matthews replies straightaway, 'It's the constipation. Janice won't go to the loo for days, then of course she's in terrible pain when she finally does go. And then she has stomach aches as well. We've taken her to the doctor and he just says it's all about Sachin and Janice'll get over it. I'm at my wits' end!'

Cameron

Cameron is three years old and was born when his mother, Becky, was in her late teens. Becky has tried to continue her own life and, although there have been no concrete worries about Cameron, the children's centre has not had much success in trying to get Becky to understand the perspective of her son.

This summer she went on holiday to Greece with a new boyfriend and left Cameron for three weeks with some friends. Cameron was very distressed while Becky was gone and has been loath to let her out of his sight ever since. Becky finds this very irritating and continues to say that she explained everything to her son and it was not a suitable holiday for a child – 'So what was I supposed to do?', she asked.

Cameron does not seem to like his mother's new boyfriend but Becky says that her son is only jealous and does not like sharing her. You have noticed that Cameron is quieter than he used to be. He has wanted to stand up to 'pee' rather than sit on the seat and one day said to you, 'I hold my willy, don't I? Nobody else should hold my willy?' Cameron was unwilling to say anymore but you also overheard him saying to one of the other boys, 'Does your Daddy hold your willy?' Sometimes the new boyfriend comes with Becky to pick up Cameron from the centre and Cameron refuses to take his hand. This afternoon it is just the boyfriend, without Becky, and Cameron has refused point blank to leave.

SAJIDA

Sajida is seven years old and attends your after-school club which is linked to her primary school. Sajida has Down's syndrome and her development is closer to that of a four-year-old. She has a helper, Amy, who stays with her during school time but does not attend the club. Your impression is that Sajida's mother still has difficulty in reconciling herself to having a disabled child and speaks with much more enthusiasm about her son, who is nearly five years old. You have never met her father.

Sajida seems to have a lot of accidents, both at school and at home. Within the last year, she has had a badly twisted ankle, a fractured arm and numerous bruises. Each time there has been a reasonable explanation and Sajida's mother and Amy agree that the child is very clumsy. You have seen Sajida bump into tables and sometimes other children, but she has never sustained more than a very mild bruise at the after-school club.

Today Sajida arrived at the club with Amy, who said that the child had slipped in the school toilets and hit her head on the taps. Sajida has a large swelling and bruise over one eye and a reddened area on one arm, where Amy says she tried to grab the child to prevent her fall. Later this afternoon, you are sympathising with Sajida, saying, 'You have a lot of bangs, don't you? How did you slip?' Sajida looks puzzled and you say, 'Amy says you slipped over in the toilet.' Sajida shakes her head and says, 'No, didn't slip. Amy banged me.'

2

How Child Protection Works

The legal framework

The changes in child protection over the last few decades are due in part to how children are now perceived. Child care is no longer seen to be a completely private issue which remains the business of families. The view that parents, or any other relatives and carers, cannot simply deal with children as they please has become well established. Society, backed by legislation, leaves parents a considerable amount of flexibility in how they care for and raise children but does place some boundaries on family choices.

The Children Act 1989 provided a new framework for the care of children and is the key piece of legislation relevant to child protection in England and Wales. The description in this chapter follows the requirements of the Children Act and related guidance. The Children (Scotland) Act 1995 and The Children (Northern Ireland) Order of 1996 cover similar ground, but have differences. Readers based in Scotland or Northern Ireland will need to check the fine details of their system.

The Children Act 1989 is a piece of **primary legislation**: it lays out the detail of the law but does not give the details of everyday practice. So the Children Act is supported by **guidance** issued by the Department of Health. Guidance does not have the force of law and details can be challenged, but usually the details of guidance are expected to be followed in professional practice. The relevant official publications in child protection are as follows:

- The Department of Health (1991) *The Children Act 1989 Guidance and Regulations – volume 2 Family support, day care and educational provision for young children* (HMSO). This guidance (known as 'The Blue Book' because of its cover) details good practice in the support services which can be used for children in need as well as for children who are not judged to be at any risk. Your own early years setting will be covered by this guidance if you work in a day nursery, children's or family centre, playgroup (often now called preschool) or an after-school club.

- If you work in a nursery class or school you will be covered by educational legislation and the specific Department for Education and Employment Circular 10/95, *Protecting children from abuse: the role of the education service.*
- The Home Office, Department of Health, Department for Education and Employment and the Welsh Office jointly issued, in 1996, *Working together under the Children Act 1989: a guide to arrangements for inter-agency co-operation for the protection of children from abuse* (HMSO). This guidance is specifically relevant to how agencies and professionals work together and confirms the fact that they should be working in co-operation.
- The Home Office (1993) *Safe from harm: a code of practice for safeguarding the welfare of children in voluntary organisations in England and Wales* (Home Office Publications). This guidance addresses issues arising in voluntary, rather than statutory services.
- The Department of Health (1988) *Protecting children: a guide for social workers undertaking a comprehensive assessment* (HMSO), also known as 'The Orange book'. This is the definitive guidance for social workers involved in child protection.

The Children Act 1989 is a law about child care and family support in the broadest sense and Part V relates specifically to child protection. Unless it falls within the education system, your own early years setting will be registered and inspected under the requirements of the Children Act. (There have been a number of Acts of this name; the text here refers exclusively to the Children Act 1989.)

The Children Act established some key principles that should underpin all practice with children:

- The welfare of the child must be paramount in any work with a family; this is known as the paramountcy principle.
- Work must be conducted in partnership. Professionals are expected to work together and to work in a co-operative way with parents.
- Children are not the possessions of their parents. Parents have responsibilities for their children, not absolute rights.

So, children have rights independently of their parents, not only through their parents. The Department of Health (DoH) guidelines state emphatically that:

> *Where there is a conflict of interests between the parents and the child, the child's interests must be given first consideration.*
> (DoH, *Protecting children: a guide for social workers undertaking a comprehensive assessment*, HMSO, 1988.)

ACTIVITY

As an early years worker, you need to know how your work could fit into the broader context of child protection and how the system operates in your local area. Local authorities have to organise the steps in the process as required by the guidance (described on page 37), but there are minor local differences, including how open professionals are to the important contribution of early years workers. You need to know, and have easily to hand, the names and contact addresses of all the professionals who form your local child protection system.

1 Ideally your local authority should provide a straightforward summary leaflet that shows you your role in the child protection process. Find the material in your setting and read it. Use the information to start your own folder on child protection in your area. Note down any questions that you would like to explore.
2 You may not have easy access to such a leaflet. Perhaps you are working in a private nursery that is not fully integrated into the local network. You could see if any other early years settings, for instance a local family centre or school, have such material.
3 If no such material exists locally, then arrange to visit a member of the local child protection team or a duty social worker. You could use the material in this chapter to guide your questions as you fill in the local details.

Steps in child protection

These steps are not negotiable or dependent on local authorities' preferences; the procedures are laid down by the Department of Health in *Working Together* and local authorities must follow them. The guidance also lays out time limits on the steps in the process; it is not allowed to drag on indefinitely.

Step 1: Initial concern and referral

The child protection process is started when someone expresses concern about the welfare of a child. This concern may be expressed from one or more of the following sources:

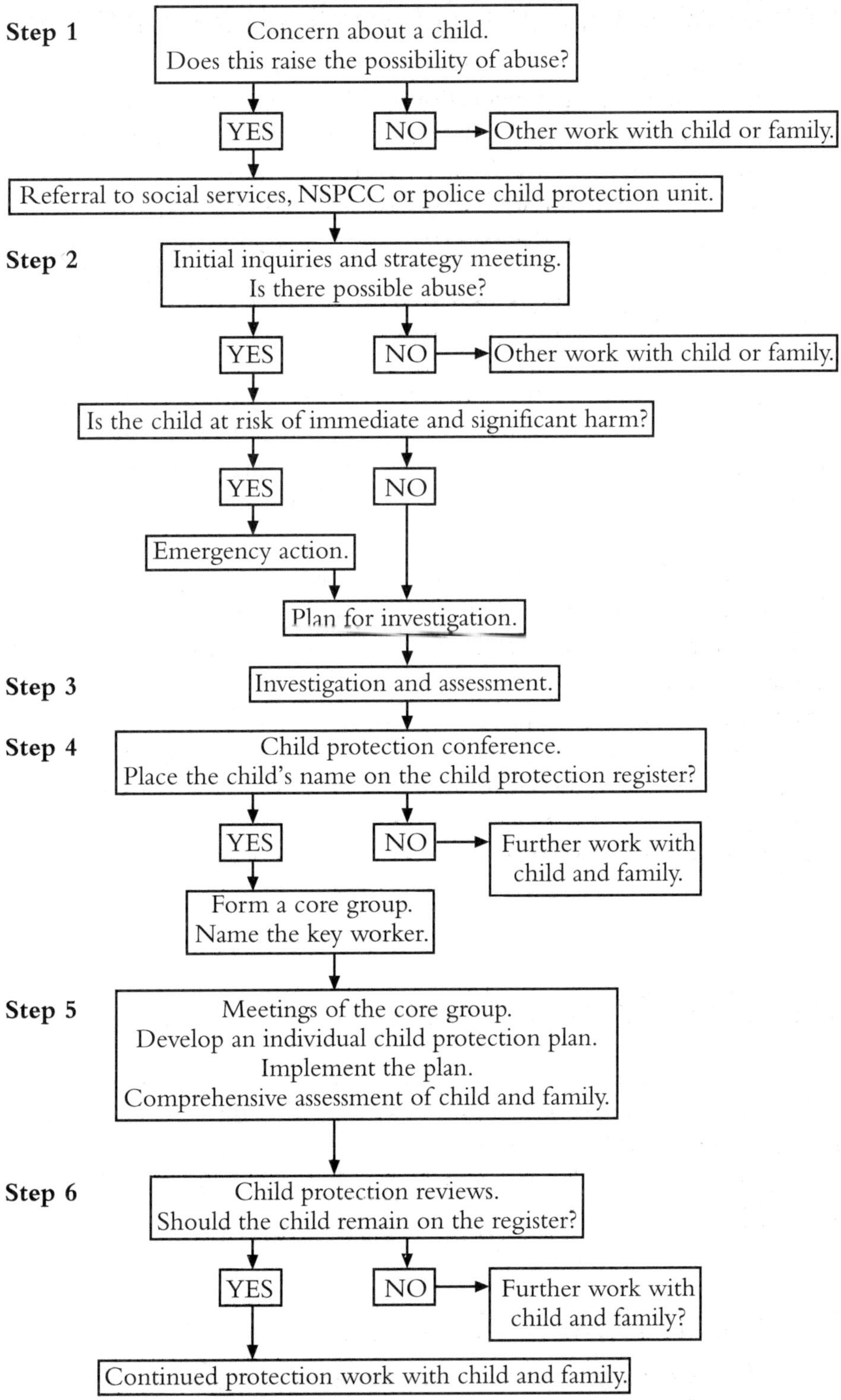
Step 1
Concern about a child.
Does this raise the possibility of abuse?
YES
NO
Other work with child or family.
Referral to social services, NSPCC or police child protection unit.
Step 2
Initial inquiries and strategy meeting.
Is there possible abuse?
YES
NO
Other work with child or family.
Is the child at risk of immediate and significant harm?
YES
NO
Emergency action.
Plan for investigation.
Step 3
Investigation and assessment.
Step 4
Child protection conference.
Place the child's name on the child protection register?
YES
NO
Further work with child and family.
Form a core group.
Name the key worker.
Step 5
Meetings of the core group.
Develop an individual child protection plan.
Implement the plan.
Comprehensive assessment of child and family.
Step 6
Child protection reviews.
Should the child remain on the register?
YES
NO
Further work with child and family?
Continued protection work with child and family.

Summary of the steps in the process of child protection

- Professionals within the health services such as a family's GP, the health visitor, a school nurse or any other specialist health professional involved with a child and his/her family.
- For younger children, early years care and education workers may be the first people to voice worries about the health, development or safety of a child. In the case of older children, concerns may be expressed by staff in the child's school, after-school club or other facilities that a child attends regularly.
- Child protection concerns may be raised by social workers themselves.
- It is not always professionals who first voice worries about a child. Some child protection inquiries are started as the result of fears for a child communicated by members of the child's own immediate family, other relatives, friends or neighbours.

Child protection concerns might then be communicated to the local social services department, the police or the local NSPCC. The local police will probably have a special unit for child protection called the Family Protection Unit (FPU) or the Child Protection Unit or Team (CPU or CPT). The NSPCC are more active in some local child protection systems than others, but the organisation has a legal right to take proceedings under the Children Act.

Step 2: Initial inquiries and strategy

Any concern regarding the possible abuse of a child has to be considered and an initial investigation made. The steps in the child protection process are intended to be steady as well as timely. The aim is that any concerns are checked carefully but that no further measures are taken unless it is judged necessary. At the start of any investigation, a decision has to be made as to whether the inquiries will be carried out by the social services on their own or whether the investigation will be a joint one, also involving the police and possibly an NSPCC social worker.

There has to be an initial strategy meeting to plan any future investigation and at this point there are three possible courses of action:

1 On the basis of the information available, it is decided not to go further with the child protection process for this child. This decision does not mean that the child and any concerns are ignored. Other possible work with the child and family may be discussed but the judgement is that there are no current child protection concerns. Not all enquiries lead to a child protection conference (Step 4).

2 It is decided that the case requires investigation on the basis of child protection concerns. Initial plans will then be made for an investigation and assessment.
3 The third possibility is that the risk to the child(ren) is judged to be so great that steps must be taken immediately. The investigation and other steps in the process will also be undertaken, but the child is judged to be at serious and immediate risk and action cannot be delayed.

Immediate Measures of Protection

The principles guiding child protection stress that professionals must act in the best interests of the child, but not take more action than is necessary. If the child cannot be protected, given all the facts of the nature of the risk (who, what, where, when and how?), then the child is judged to be at risk of significant harm. Action can then be taken under the Children Act to protect him/her from immediate danger. Such steps are not taken lightly and are not used in many child protection cases. The general principles of legal process under the Children Act apply here; these are that:

- The welfare of the child must be the prime concern – S.1.(1).
- The aim is to avoid and reduce delay that would be prejudicial to the welfare of the child – S.1.(2).
- There is to be no court order (emergency, or other kinds of order) unless making an order is clearly better for the child – S.1.(5). Court orders are not to be used as a matter of routine.

If a court order is necessary, then there are two choices:

- Under the Children Act (S.2., para 5.1. to 5.6.), an **Emergency Protection Order** can be taken out by social services or by the NSPCC. This order is only allowed when there is an immediate risk to the child and social workers are required to make a case to the court when they apply for the order. The order will be granted if the child is not safe at home, the parent(s) will not permit the voluntary removal of the child and there is nowhere for the child to be kept safe with the parents' consent. The effect of an Emergency Protection Order is to compel a parent, or other relevant person, to produce the child and allow the local authority to remove him/her to a place of safety. The order can also be used to prevent the removal of a child by parents or other persons from a place that is judged to be safe for the child. The court can additionally issue a warrant authorising a police officer to assist in the removal of the child, or in preventing his/her removal.

- Alternatively, under the Children Act (S.2., para 5.7.), the police have the powers to remove the child to suitable alternative accommodation or to prevent the child being removed from a specific place.

DEVELOPING A PLAN FOR INVESTIGATION

The initial strategy meeting must plan the investigation, if the decision is to proceed with a child protection inquiry. The details have to be decided on the basis of the information available so far, the different strands of the investigation that have to be followed up and the other professionals involved with the family. It has to be clear who will be responsible for conducting the investigation and making contact with the child, family and other involved agencies. The strategy meeting basically assesses the evidence so far. It is possible that, at this point, the police representative might say that there is insufficient evidence to suggest a possible criminal prosecution in the future and will not be involved further in the process for this child.

UNDERSTANDING THE ROLE OF THE POLICE

The work of the police in the child protection process is rather different from that of other professionals. They can only justify their continuing involvement with a child protection case on two, related grounds:

- That if the abuse is proven, then the abuser(s) will be proved to have committed a crime. The alleged actions have to fall within one of the possible categories that define a crime under law.
- There has to be sufficient evidence that a prosecution is likely to succeed. The police pass on the evidence to the Crown Prosecution Service (CPS) who make the final decision on whether to go ahead with criminal proceedings.

If the police withdraw from the child protection process, it does not mean that they believe the abuse of this child does not matter, nor that they think someone is mistaken or lying. It means that either there is no identifiable crime, however powerful the information collected, or that the evidence collected so far has been judged by the CPS as too weak to stand up in court. Of course, some cases do go to trial and, for various reasons, do not result in a prosecution. It is important that you understand the limits placed on the police force, since you may be supporting both parents and children who have unrealistic hopes that a recognised abuser will definitely be prosecuted.

Generally speaking, the police are only involved in a child protection case when there is possible physical or sexual abuse, since the actions of the abuser may, but will not definitely, constitute a crime. Emotional abuse is frequently very hard to prove and does not produce evidence that falls into the category of a crime. So police involvement continuing through the child protection process is very unlikely if emotional abuse is the only strand in the investigation. But it is important to realise, for yourself and in supporting parents and children, that very serious steps can be taken on behalf of a child at risk whether there is an identifiable crime or not. The possibilities for child protection under the Children Act do not require proof that a crime has taken place (see page 39).

Step 3: Investigation and assessment

A full investigation has to be carried out after the strategy meeting and before the child protection conference. This investigation is carried out under Section 47 of the Children Act and is a necessary part of the later case conference (Step 4) when it is decided whether or not to place the child's name on the child protection register. A child cannot be registered without this prior investigation.

Guidance under the Children Act has established that the prime tasks of a child protection investigation are to:

- Establish the facts about the circumstances giving rise to the concern.
- Identify whether there are grounds to consider that the child is or is not likely to suffer significant harm.
- Identify the sources and levels of risks.
- Decide on the necessary protective and other actions in relation to the child.
- Secure by interview or medical examination the evidence from which a decision can be made regarding civil or criminal proceedings (the difference between these is explained on page 142).

The principles of an investigation are that it should:

- Always be child-centred and any procedures should be undertaken with the child's feelings and experiences in mind. Interviews or examinations should be explained and undertaken with consideration, avoiding further distress to an already hurt or confused child.
- Have due regard to the legal requirements. However concerned professionals may be about a child, they must act within the law.
- Involve parents and carers in the whole process unless it can be clearly justified as prejudicial to the investigation. For instance, parents might be excluded if they continually disrupt meetings or intimidate the child.

In these cases the parents' views should still be sought and they should be given information. If parents refuse to co-operate in the investigation, a Child Assessment Order can be obtained, under the Children Act, to compel some co-operation and allow assessment of the child.
- Fully assess the child's circumstances before any action is taken.
- Undertake interviews with an open mind, having regard to different child care practices but with the welfare of the child as central.

Step 4: The child protection conference

Not all child protection concerns reach this stage. The whole point of initial inquiries and the investigation is to ensure that further steps are not taken unless there is genuine cause for concern.

The child protection conference brings together any professionals with relevant information to share, and the family itself. The conference has to be called no more than 10 days after the concern has first been lodged. A child protection conference is attended by some, but not necessarily all, of the following people (representatives from different professions are not invited unless they are involved with the family or have a direct contribution to make):

- A social worker will definitely be present.
- The parent(s) will be invited.
- A residential social worker or family centre worker.
- The police, represented by the liaison officer from the Family Protection Unit, or the investigating officer.
- A medical professional such as the family's GP or the school nurse.
- A representative from education or day care – a teacher, head teacher, early years worker or educational psychologist.
- If relevant, someone from the Probation Department.
- A local NSPCC social worker.
- The County Secretary and Solicitor.

Studies of the child protection process have suggested that co-operation between different professionals is most likely at the beginning of the process and at the investigation stage. Social workers are the most likely profession to carry on with the work.

The Involvement of Parents

The Children Act and the Department of Health guidelines firmly stress that parents should remain a part of the child protection process. Parents must be invited to the case conference, unless it can be shown that there is a very good reason why they should not be there, and one or both parents might be excluded if they are likely to become violent or very disruptive. Parents are not compelled to attend; they have a choice. At the case conference, parents can hear the views of everyone else and they can contribute their own views. However, they do not participate in the conference decision making.

A professional involved in a case conference must understand what the parents might be feeling. It is a very stressful experience, as is the entire investigation. Parents can feel outnumbered around the table and especially threatened if the police are present – as they will be if the suspected abuse could lead to criminal prosecution.

The Child Protection Register

The conference decides, on the basis of the evidence, whether to place the child on the local child protection register. The register is maintained by the local social services on behalf of all the agencies involved in working with children who have been abused, or who are judged as being at risk of abuse, and for whom there is a need for a child protection plan. It is also possible for the NSPCC to maintain the register on behalf of the local authority.

Children can be put on the register as early as birth, or even before birth, but there would have to be sufficient evidence for such a move. The key point is that children whose names are placed on the register are judged to be at risk of abuse. The children have not necessarily been abused already, but all the information gathered for the case conference leads to the decision that abuse is a real possibility. However, in some cases, there may be very strong indications that the children have already been abused.

Children can only be placed on the register if the criteria for registration are met:

- There must have been one or more identifiable incident(s) that can be described as having adversely affected the child. These incidents might be something that was done to a child, or failures to act on behalf of a child.
- The professional judgement is that further incidents involving this child are likely.
- The abuse must be categorised under one, or more, of the four types: neglect, physical injury, sexual abuse or emotional abuse (refer to Chapter 1 for definitions of these).

If a child is not placed on the register, there may still be further work to be undertaken with the family, led by the relevant social worker or carried out in an early years setting. The investigation will be written up in the family's file but no further steps will be taken within the child protection process.

If the child's name is placed on the register, other actions must now follow:

- A core group is formed of the professionals most involved with the family. This group will not be very large (see under Step 5 for more details).
- A key worker must be identified by name and this person will take primary responsibility for the case. The key worker is often a social worker, but it could be the family centre worker in settings that have been organised to deal with families under stress.
- A child protection plan must be developed specifically for this child.

Usually, there is only one child protection conference and the work is continued by the core group. Another case conference would only be called if there was evidence that procedures had not been followed properly, or if it became clear that all the relevant information for the decision had not been shared at the time of the first conference.

THE CHILD PROTECTION PLAN

In good practice, professionals do not focus most of their energy on identification and investigation of children at risk. Children will be protected and helped through actions that follow. When faced with children at risk, the professionals involved have several options:

- They can start a child protection inquiry under Section 47 of the Children Act 1989. A comprehensive assessment of the child will often be important to identify how best to help. The earlier investigation is only to establish whether the child is being abused or at risk of abuse and does not necessarily point to what to do about the abuse and risk.
- They can look at the possibilities within family support services under Section 17 of the Act.
- They can consider the child welfare services, including a placement in a community or foster home.

These options are not necessarily on an either/or basis. A Section 47 inquiry often leads to the use of the Section 17 services to safeguard or promote the child's welfare through the family support services. Actions might include attending a family centre, home support for parents or placement of the child in an early years setting.

Early years workers and parents are often worried that a child protection investigation is likely to mean children are taken away from their families. But this is an unusual course of action, because guidelines stress that children are to be left with their families, unless there is clear evidence that their welfare can only be safeguarded away from home.

Only in exceptional circumstances will social workers take emergency action under Part V of the Act and remove children to a foster family or residential home. Social workers can use Care and Supervision Orders to make the children the responsibility of the local authority if children are judged to be suffering, or likely to suffer significant harm, are not receiving reasonable care or are out of parental control. Recovery Orders can be used if there is reason to believe that a child has been abducted or taken away from those who have parental responsibility. Sometimes parents agree voluntarily that the child(ren) might be looked after for a period of time – this is known as the child welfare route.

Discussion and reviews of child protection practice have expressed concern that emphasis is too often placed on investigation, rather than on intervention through family support. Good practice is seen as a process that blends Section 47 inquiries with the provision of Section 17 services. Some local authorities have looked carefully at how to shift practice towards an integrated child protection and family support work system, in which early action and preventative work is stressed more than swift reactions when a crisis point is reached in a family.

Step 5: Meetings of the core group

The core group will consist of the key worker, probably a social worker, and other professionals directly relevant to this family. The group also includes the parent(s) and the children, if they are judged to be old enough to be involved. As with the child protection conference, there must be a very good reason for not inviting the parent(s).

The core group meets on a regular basis (fortnightly) and has to develop and carry out detailed plans, including:

- Developing the child protection plan, which includes the need to identify objective criteria about protection for this child.

- Implementing the child protection plan.
- Ensuring that there is a comprehensive assessment of the child and family. At the case conference it was only decided that, on the basis of the initial investigation, there is cause to put the child's name on the register.
- Ensuring that all the elements of the plan are implemented.
- Setting up a matrix, which is a pattern of formal monitoring of the child's welfare and well-being. The matrix lays out who will see the child on which day of the week.

ASSESSMENT OF THE CHILD

A comprehensive assessment of the child forms part of the child protection plan. This action includes gathering information from all the agencies who know the child and family and can include a developmental and/or medical assessment of the child. Any assessment must also include the child's own views and wishes.

Good practice is that any assessment directly involving the child, whether a developmental assessment, an interview or a medical examination, must be undertaken with respectful concern for the child, both in terms of their physical care and their feelings. No assessment, at this stage or at the earlier investigation stage, should further add to a child's distress or feelings of being used or abused. Any collection of evidence should always be balanced against avoiding further trauma to the child. Some child abuse inquiries have made the specific point that children should not be subject to repetitive and long interviews, nor to repeated medical examinations.

Medical examinations do not always form a part of the assessment of children at risk. A medical examination of a child is undertaken for specific reasons, such as to:

- Detect traumatic or infectious conditions.
- Evaluate the nature of the abuse.
- Provide evidence including forensic proof.
- Provide a developmental assessment that could provide a benchmark on the child's failure to thrive.
- Reassure a child who fears that the abuse has seriously damaged him physically.
- Start the process of recovery for an abused child.

A medical examination, including the use of X-rays, does not always produce clear-cut results, for instance, about how an injury was caused or whether it was accidental or non-accidental, beyond 'reasonable doubt'.

A comprehensive assessment is presented at the first child protection review meeting, or, less often, at a reconvened case conference (see page 44). The core group is responsible for taking action on the basis of the assessment, always bearing in mind the child's wishes, feelings and perceptions.

Step 6: Reviews

Children do not remain on the child protection register for ever. Every six months there must be a review, the aim of which is to assess whether the child's name should remain on the register. This review is attended by all those with relevant information, including the parents and the child(ren), if they are old enough.

Deregistration

The child's name is taken off the register under the following possible circumstances:

- The original factors that led to registration no longer apply:
  - the child is still at home but the risk is reduced through work with the family
  - the child is away from home and the source of the risk
  - the abusing adult or young person has gone
  - assessment and analysis shows that child protection is not necessary
- The child and family have left the area and the area to which they have moved has assumed responsibility for the case.
- The child at risk is no longer deemed to be a child: s/he has either reached the age of legal majority (18 years) or has got married (between 16 and 18 years).
- The child has died.

If the review decides that the child's name will be taken off the register, work can continue with the child and family, involving whichever professionals are appropriate. The child and family may still need help but the child is no longer judged to be at risk.

How well does the system work?

Lessons from public inquiries

A special case management review must follow the death or very serious injury of a child whenever child abuse is confirmed or suspected. The deaths of children while the local authority is involved with the family have sometimes led to more public inquiries and reports. The changes brought about by the death of Maria Colwell in 1974 are described on page 2, but subsequent tragedies have brought the names of other children into the public arena. The separate deaths of Jasmine Beckford, Tyra Henry, Kimberley Carlile and Leanne White may be familiar to you, but other children have died or been very seriously injured and their cases have not been reported nationally.

There have also been public inquiries following investigations into child abuse when opinions have been divided, for instance, in the sexual abuse cases in Cleveland, Rochdale and the Orkneys. Inquiries also usually follow the discovery of substantial abuse at residential institutions or day care settings – for instance, the physically abusive 'Pindown' system used by Tony Latham in Staffordshire children's homes, or the Kincora children's homes scandal in Northern Ireland.

Public inquiries address the particular circumstances surroundings a child's death or the discovery of large-scale abuse. The impact of high profile cases is to unsettle everyone, not only those in that area. The experience of tragedy or the discovery of professional misconduct can shake general morale and confidence, yet the inquiries highlight issues for good practice that needed to be addressed. The Department of Health has commissioned reviews to identify the practice implications of the series of inquiries mentioned above. The key points that have emerged are also relevant for early years workers as they consider their role within the process of child protection.

FOCUS ON THE CHILD(REN)

It is very important to be aware of the state and development of children as individuals in their own right. In some cases that ended in tragedy for the child, professional attention seemed, with hindsight, to be too focused on the parents' problems and experience of stress. The needs of children should never be overlooked in order to maintain a good relationship with parents, or any other adults. A criticism made in the inquiry on the Cleveland sex abuse cases was that the children themselves ran the risk of being lost in the flurry of diagnosis and counter-claim. A telling phrase from that report is now often quoted: 'The child is a person, not an object of concern.'

PROFESSIONALS MUST WORK WELL TOGETHER

Inquiries have stressed the great importance of inter-agency working: that all the professionals involved with a child and/or family must discuss, consult and share information in such a way as to protect the child. Some inquiries have highlighted the dangers for children if their protection is weakened by unclear boundaries for inter-agency work. Relationships between the different professionals and the levels of their intervention need to be guided by written procedures. Some inquiries have pointed to competition and hostility between professionals as one reason for the mis-management of a case. It is true that arguments between professionals are unproductive, but it must also be remembered that a failure to raise issues can be just as dangerous.

More than one inquiry has pointed out the necessity of using observations and assessment by people who see child(ren) regularly. If all the different reports and knowledge of children are brought together, then the seriousness of a situation may be more obvious. This finding suggests the value of consulting early years settings where children are seen on a regular basis, sometimes daily. However, the child protection system still does not explicitly involve early years settings, unless they are part of a school.

Avoid Unrealistic Optimism

Adults would often rather think well of other adults – that they would not deliberately harm their children or place children's needs at the bottom of their list of priorities. Yet no professional can afford to be guided by what has been called 'the rule of optimism': the wish to think the best of people. It is equally as important not to be unduly pessimistic about a family, and certainly not to work on unsupported assumptions of likely failure because of the family's social, ethnic or religious identity. However, some inquiries have pointed to the risks that followed from professionals' over-optimism that a parent, or other adult, could cope, or that the parent's view of the situation was the most reliable.

Maintain a Professional Objectivity

Professionals within any of the branches of social, family and child care have to maintain a balance between caring and detachment. They have to avoid becoming over-involved with the family and overlooking the needs of the child(ren) in order to protect a working relationship with the parents. No worker should resist acting on concerns about children because 'it could damage my relationship with the parents'. There are serious risks if professionals do become over-involved. They may overlook the significance of family patterns of behaviour because they are focusing on single events or crises. These risks are multiplied if the child protection worker is operating without sufficient support.

THE CRUCIAL NEED FOR SUPPORT

No worker should operate in child protection without clear lines of support. All workers, but especially those who are less experienced, need easy access to supervision. The judgements and decisions that need to be made in child protection are rarely straightforward and consultation and the consideration of different perspectives are crucial. Good quality supervision and professional support should also offer a way of dealing with personal feelings and values, including cultural and religious issues. Concerns about a family need to be acknowledged as do any worries about the professional's own personal safety with a particular family.

A BALANCE BETWEEN INVESTIGATION AND FAMILY SUPPORT

A recurring dilemma when child abuse concerns arise is deciding at what point to start an investigation into a family, institution or individual. In the second half of the 1990s there was a shift towards what was called the 'lighter touch': trying to explore possibilities of family support and not moving too quickly into the investigation process. This has been called the 'refocusing debate' and has worked to find a new balance in the child protection system between using the investigation sections of the Children Act 1989 and family support.

How might you be involved?

Practice varies considerably between different areas, but, in general, there is a stronger tradition of involving schools and teachers than early years settings like playgroups or day nurseries. It is hard to explain this division unless you link it to the general care/education divide and the view that school staff are professionals and early years workers are generally not. I disagree with this view, but it exists and influences the poor practice that can leave early years settings out of the child protection process.

The Department for Education and Employment Circular 10/95 requires local authority and grant-maintained schools to have procedures for child protection and a designated member of staff responsible for co-ordinating work between the school and other agencies. The local social services has a duty to inform a school if a child on the school roll is placed on the child protection register, or if the child starts school. The school must monitor the child's attendance and development and report any concerns to the local education authority. It is also the school's responsibility to inform the keeper of the child protection register if the child changes school.

There are no equivalent expectations of non-educational early years settings, nor a requirement that the setting be informed in the same way as schools. You may be involved by your local team, but there is no official line similar to the position if you work in a nursery or primary school. You are more likely to be involved, however, if you work in settings that have a selected population that brings in more families who are deemed to be at risk and children who are 'in need', for instance, in family centres or local authority children's centres.

Nevertheless, two strong themes in good practice in child protection make it likely that early years settings will be more involved in the child protection process:

1 Inquiries and guidelines stress that the focus on the child must never be lost in concerns about adults within the family. Early years settings have worked hard to develop partnerships with parents alongside a clear focus on children and their development. Early years settings usually keep developmental records of children and see them on a regular basis, sometimes daily.
2 Reviews of practice continue to emphasise that professionals must work together and social workers, or other key workers in a core group, must draw on all the agencies involved with a child and family. This will often include early years settings.

Possibilities of Involvement

An early years centre can have an important role to play in child protection but needs to be clear about what should be done internally and what should be referred to the appropriate person. No early years worker, however senior in the setting, will undertake an investigation, as described on page 38. This is the job of the social worker. However, there are a number of equally important ways in which you might be involved in the child protection process:

- Concerns might be raised first within your centre. You are in an important position to be aware of the development and well-being of individual children. Good practice in any early years setting is to keep records of children's attendance and of their developmental progress. So, you may be the first professional to become concerned about a child's failure to thrive physically, difficulties in development or the changing behaviour of a previously happy child.
- Early years workers do not have to make the judgement whether a concern about a child is enough to indicate that the child is being

abused. You would never start a child protection investigation yourself but the centre could be crucial at the early stage of exploring the seriousness of a concern.

- Your first awareness of a problem might be when you are contacted by a social worker or child protection co-ordinator because concerns have been raised elsewhere about a child who attends your centre.
- If a child is on the local child protection register then the social services may inform and involve your setting, even though it is not a school. You may be asked to monitor this child's attendance and development and report any concerns to the social worker in charge of the case. You might be asked to tell a social worker immediately if a child fails to arrive as agreed or if the parent intends to move the child to another setting.
- Your usual written records of children and their development will be important for a child who is at risk but you may also keep other factual records (see page 103) including exchanges with the child and parent(s).
- You might be asked to be present when a child is being interviewed regarding concerns about possible abuse. When you know a child well, your presence might be very reassuring through what could otherwise be a confusing or distressing experience.
- You, or your head of centre, may present reports at a case conference or later review of the case.
- Work with the child and the parent(s) in the centre may be a specific part of the child protection plan that is developed when the child's name is added to the child protection register. Certainly, placement of the child in an early years setting should not be the end of the work with the family. The key social worker should remain in contact with you.
- You may have an important role to play in supporting parents and continuing to work with them at the centre. Some families may work more closely with the duty social worker but some parents may have developed a good working relationship with you; a parent may turn to you for explanations or appreciate your company at the case conference.
- It is possible, although unlikely, that you may be called upon to give evidence in criminal proceedings (see page 144). Most abuse cases do not reach the courts, so only a few readers of this book will ever experience being a witness.

3

Policies, Procedures and Good Practice

Early years settings have a very important role to play in a comprehensive approach to child protection. Workers within the different kinds of centres have regular contact with children and their parents. Child protection should not be seen as a purely internal concern but neither is it a matter just for outside specialists such as social workers. The part early years workers play in child protection requires the following:

- Knowledge and understanding of the whole framework of which you are a part (Chapter 2 describes the child protection system as a whole).
- Understanding of the role of early years workers: how you could be involved, as well as what you will *not* be doing.
- Knowledge of the policy and procedures of your setting: what you do in your centre and what is expected of you as part of your job.

Policy and procedures

Good practice in early years work involves clear, public policies. A policy on child protection is part of the work of any early years centre, regardless of the children and families who use your service. In the different aspects of your work **policies** lay out the key principles that should guide and inform your work and **procedures** describe the details of the steps that should be followed. It is likely that your child protection guidance may include principles and action within the same material. Consequently, this text refers to written guidance as child protection procedures.

Procedures on child protection should be in place as a matter of good practice. You do not, for instance, wait for children to have accidents in your settings before you decide on procedures on first aid. All your staff should know where the first aid materials are kept and the safe steps to follow when dealing with a minor or more serious injury. In the same way, it would be very poor practice if a centre postponed any consideration of child protection until a crisis developed.

You are not, of course, trying to assess whether the kinds of families you meet are likely to abuse their children. There are no easy predictions in child protection, because no one can say with confidence that particular people are likely, or unlikely, to abuse or neglect their children. Additionally, families that have taken good care of their children can be shocked to find that someone else, trusted by the family, has abused the children. So detailed procedures should be in place whatever the area you work in, the families who use your service or the kind of service you offer. As with any other policy on good practice, the guidance on child protection in your setting should be drafted so that it is straightforward to use:

- The procedures should be written down in a format that is easy to consult and understand for all team members, including volunteers. The concerns and guidance for action apply to everyone.
- The procedures should be public, in that they should be available for consultation by parents or any professionals involved with the centre.
- Key issues in child protection should be communicated to parents as part of establishing a good working relationship between families and the centre. So, for instance, general material about the centre and initial conversations with parents are an opportunity to communicate that you have obligations to report and address concerns about children.
- Any policy should be open to discussion and review. Certainly if you are drafting a policy for the first time, it is a good idea to set a date, perhaps six months ahead, when the policy will be discussed in detail and sensible revisions made.

Child protection procedures

Procedures need to be worded and communicated in a positive way, as you do not want to give the impression that all parents, workers or volunteers in the centre are seen as potential abusers. Such an approach would be very destructive and would not reflect the genuine level of risk for children – the huge majority of adults do not abuse children. The procedures need to be presented positively as part of how you care for children and as a reflection of your awareness that child abuse is a reality within our society. The procedures should make clear your responsibilities within the broader framework of child care and education, and emphasise that members of the centre team are accountable for their own actions.

Your centre's child protection procedures should lay out clearly the responsibilities of the centre and its staff, including:

- Responsibilities as regards child protection: duties under a legal framework that affect everyone in child care, early education and playwork.
- The duty of staff to work towards prevention of child abuse and to react appropriately to any concerns.
- A summary of signs that should concern a worker, but which are not necessarily proof of child abuse.
- What to do when workers have concerns and what not to do. The role of an early years worker is to deal with the immediate situation involving a child or adult and to pass on concerns. Procedures should make clear the difference between talking with a child or parent and undertaking an investigation (which is the role of a social worker).
- The steps that will be followed when there is reason for concern; the balance between confidentiality and the centre's obligation to pass on concerns.
- The ways in which an early years worker might be involved as a contributor to a child protection investigation.
- Ways of supporting a child, and parent, who is involved in the child protection process.
- Details of who should be consulted locally: the local social services department, a local branch of the NSPCC or the police child protection team. Procedures should make it clear who should be contacted under what circumstances, if there is a choice.
- The policy on keeping records, good practice in observation and written reports, and the policy on sharing records with parents.
- Issues of security in the setting, including who has responsibility for collecting children at the end of the day or session and visitors to the centre.
- The procedures for making checks on new workers and volunteer; a system for dealing with criticisms of staff practice, or accusations of child abuse.

Good practice in child protection involves making supported judgements about a child and your concerns about him/her. Clear child protection procedures are necessary so that everyone understands the framework in which you are working in an early years centre. But no procedure, however good, will make decisions for you. Written guidelines give you a framework in which to work and should indicate how to consult, seek support and pass on concerns appropriately. The most experienced professional in child protection still has to make carefully considered judgements based on what is known and what can reasonably be predicted.

ACTIVITY

If you are on a work placement, look at the child protection procedures of your setting.

1 Do they cover all these issues? If not, how might any gaps be covered?
2 How often are the procedures updated with changes in the names and contact numbers of people who should be contacted?
3 If your setting has no proper procedures then consult an appropriate draft. Some of the organisations for early years have useful booklets – see the addresses from page 179.

If you are not on a work placement, discuss the above with your tutor.

A simple plan of action summarising the procedures might help workers who are concerned about a child. On page 57 there is a possible plan, but it will not suit all places or situations. Use this draft to reach an appropriate plan for your own setting.

Any written policy and procedures documents should be available in the main languages spoken in your area. For some early years settings, this task may be very straightforward, but if you work in a diverse area in which many languages are spoken, the translation task may be daunting. This issue will arise with all written material originating from the centre, so you may need to contact local translation and interpretation services. Bilingual workers or parents may be able to help, but it would be wise to obtain a second opinion on translations, especially with sensitive subjects such as child protection.

Some parents or carers will not be literate or may be very reluctant readers, so workers should always be ready to explain orally any aspect of centre practice, and not only child protection.

Adult responsibilities

Staff behaviour

All early years settings need clear guidelines for the behaviour of workers, parent helpers, volunteers and young people on work placement. This kind of policy has links with child protection but many of the issues are about more general good practice with children. The main issues include:

- A positive approach to dealing with children's behaviour and any misbehaviour. Staff need to understand what are acceptable and unacceptable approaches to discipline (see pages 159–63).
- The standards of behaviour that are expected of staff in their work with the children and some sense of what is non-negotiable and what is more a matter for individual style.

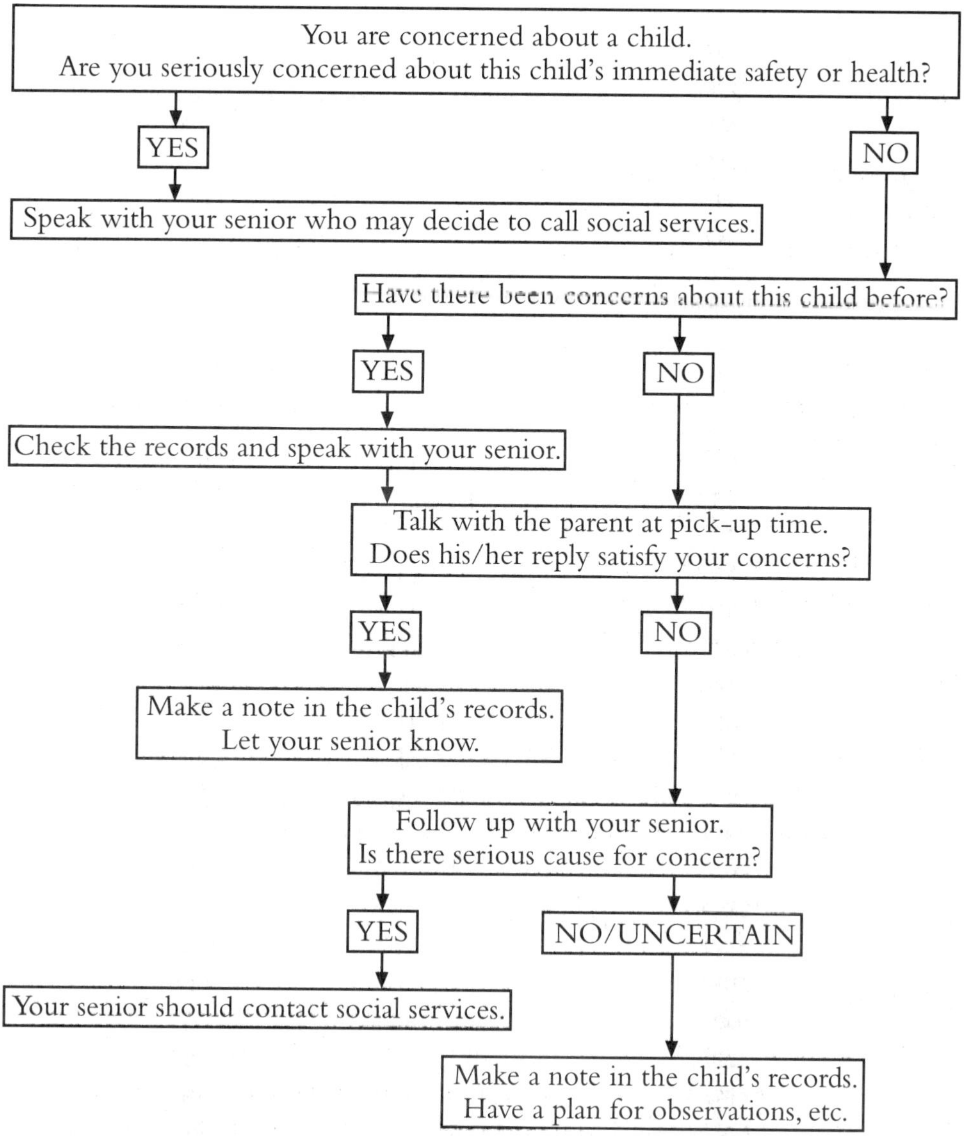

A possible procedure map for an early years or playwork setting

- All settings need to have discussed appropriate and inappropriate physical contact with children. This issue is particularly important in the physical care of young children or older disabled children (see pages 27–8). This discussion should also cover the issue of respect for children and the importance of not imposing adult needs for emotional support or affection onto the children.
- Appropriate touch is also a feature of physical contact within discipline when children may need to be restrained for their own safety or that of others.
- Senior workers and the head of centre should monitor the programme of activities for the children – what is done and how.

It is also good practice to monitor any trips that workers make with children. It should always be clear what workers have planned for a trip: where they are going and the purpose of the trip. One reason why such outings should be monitored is because some abusers within early years settings have used trips out as the opportunity to abuse children. However, the vast majority of unacceptable trips with children are not abusive in intention or result, but are simply a poor use of time with the children, such as trailing them round shops that are only of interest to adults.

ORGANISATION OF THE WORK

Attempts to organise a setting in order to minimise the chance of child abuse have to be considered realistically. Some settings have established firm ground rules to ensure that children are always with more than one person or that male workers do not undertake any intimate care of children.

In many settings, however, it is completely unrealistic to insist that there is always more than one worker present with a child or group. The recommendation unfortunately suggests that all workers are potential abusers, yet it does not remove all possibility of abuse. Single abusers are more common but abusers have been known to work with one or more colleagues. The limitations on male workers are misplaced for several reasons (see page 62).

Unfortunately, there is no definitive way of organising work that will remove all possibility of abuse within an early years setting. However, procedures for checking staff and an atmosphere in which children and adults feel able to raise concerns will go a long way to preventing abuse within the setting.

A focus on the children

The emphasis of any early years setting must always be on the children and their well-being. A setting with a strong community focus probably has to keep an especially strong hold on this perspective. The same is true of centres that offer work experience to students or other young people. An early years centre is not a therapeutic community for staff or volunteers. Nor is it the children's role to create training opportunities for adults and young people.

- The supervision system in any setting should be used to support any worker whose health or emotional well-being is leading to stress at work. But you should never lose sight of a worker's daily practice with the children. If stress, brought on by problems in the worker's home life, is leading to poor practice, then the children's safety and well-being have to be the prime concern. If a choice is forced, then the well-being of the children is more important than sympathy for adults and a wish not to upset them by challenging poor practice or changing their work duties.
- Volunteers can be welcome and may be crucial for the running of some early years settings, but no centre should tolerate bad practice from a volunteer on the grounds of 'We can't make a fuss, she's giving her time for free.' Of course, concerns about poor practice from volunteers, as with some workers, will not always be at the level of child abuse. A senior worker might have to deal with a volunteer who is regularly impatient with the children or insists on table manners that are culturally very specific and inappropriate to the centre.
- Centres are sometimes contacted by other local organisations who ask for an individual to be placed with them in order to gain experience of working with them, because working with children might help this individual. Heads of early years settings must not feel under any obligation to agree to this. A volunteer should only be accepted because s/he is a suitable person to be with children. You might have sympathy for this person's needs but your prime concern has to be whether the children will benefit.

New workers and volunteers

All prospective staff and volunteers should be thoroughly checked through a careful interviewing procedure. You should take up the references and qualifications of individuals to whom you are considering offering a job. This system will identify people who are dishonest about their qualifications and previous experience – a greater risk for most centres than employing abusers.

Police checks, for offences against children, should also be made on any person to whom you are considering offering a job. If your centre is part of a voluntary organisation, then you may be able to use the Department of Health Consultancy Service. Any early years setting registered under the Children Act 1989 can ask the local authority to undertake police checks with the local police force, who will check national as well as local records. Educational establishments can use the Department of Education List 99. Local authorities have different guidelines about police checks and you should talk to your local Under-Eights Advisor if you are at all unclear about these. Ideally you should also carry out police checks on volunteers. Your centre should make it clear to anyone who applies for a job, or offers to volunteer, that you will carry out this check and explain how and why it is done.

Paedophiles will continue to attempt to gain access to children through paid jobs or voluntary work. No checking procedures will ever be 100% safe, but sloppy systems make it easy for an abuser.

Induction and support

Checks on workers and volunteers are an important part of good practice but this is only one step in effective child protection. All workers and volunteers should have a copy of their centre's policies, and the implications for practice should be explained in detail and in more than one conversation, if necessary.

- Workers need to be clear about guidelines on good practice, for instance about a positive approach to children's behaviour, their physical care or trips out of the centre. Such support is sometimes overlooked for volunteers, but is just as necessary.
- Paid workers should have a job description but it is also a good idea to give volunteers an outline of what they are expected to do and explain to them the limits to their responsibilities.
- Workers and volunteers should know exactly how much and what support they can expect and that it is good practice to ask rather than assume, when uncertain.
- Any adult or young person who is working with the children in your centre needs to recognise that poor practice will be challenged, as indeed good practice should be encouraged. Everyone has to keep

within the good practice boundaries. It is irrelevant for the children that someone is volunteering their time or is present only for a fixed work experience slot. As with any worker, if they are gossiping about the parents or developing obvious favourites among the children, then a senior worker must challenge the behaviour.

Visitors to the centre

An early years centre will have a number of visitors, such as those who are interested in your work or people who have a legitimate involvement in the centre, for instance, members of the management committee.

Good practice in any centre is to keep track of the number of visitors, since too many adults can be a disruption to children's learning. Children, just like adults, may also resent regular unannounced arrivals of visitors. Child protection concerns arise in that visitors should be monitored and not simply left to wander about a centre. Any concerns raised by children, or their parents, about a regular visitor, should be dealt with in the same way as concerns about any other adult or young person. David Finkelhor's study of sexual abuse in day care settings in the United States established that, in something like half of the cases, the perpetrator was neither a stranger nor a member of staff, but a regular visitor to the centre.

Communication within the centre

Child protection procedures will depend on good communication within an early years setting:

- Workers should be confident that there are opportunities to talk with colleagues and senior staff and that their concerns will be taken seriously.
- Any centre needs a system of supervision and support for workers. Supervision should be in place not only because of child protection concerns but also to deal with any other worries a worker might have.
- Working with a child and family can be stressful when there are child protection concerns. The worker has to maintain confidentiality and not discuss the family outside the centre, but it is the responsibility of senior workers to ensure that the worker has the opportunity to express worries or doubts within the centre. The chance to talk should be seen as a usual part of such work and not available only 'if you're really upset'.

- Workers who are involved with children on a daily basis should be informed about what is happening in a child protection case by the senior worker, who in turn may need to ensure that the centre is kept informed by outside agencies.

Men working with young children

Early years teams have always been overwhelmingly female. It is unusual to encounter male workers in nurseries and playgroups, and primary schools usually have far more female teachers than male. The main reason for this imbalance seems to be that working with babies and young children is traditionally seen as women's work. The job has been undervalued and pay and conditions, although they have improved, still reflect these attitudes. Children's and family centres that have multi-disciplinary teams often have more men, who may join the centre with a qualification other than child care or early education. The playwork tradition links with youth and leisure work and involves working with older children. Consequently, it is more usual to meet male workers in after-school clubs or holiday schemes.

THE CHILD PROTECTION FOCUS

Until concern about child abuse came to the forefront, many early years teams were keen to encourage more male involvement in order to provide children with a well-rounded experience. However, awareness of sexual abuse has raised some difficult issues. As a consequence, some teams and local authorities have made ground rules that only apply to male workers or have refused to have any men working in early years centres. This debate is a complicated one and there are no sure answers. This section covers the main issues and will help you to think about this area of practice, whether you are female or male.

Concern about male workers with young children has arisen because of a general belief that most abusers are male, and children have to be protected. However:

- The only area of child abuse in which men predominate is sexual abuse. The impact of sexual abuse on children can be substantial, but it is not the only child protection concern. Additionally, some women have sexually abused children and, where there is institutional abuse, women are relatively more prominent than in abuse by family or friends.
- Banning men from early years work would not deal with the fact that women can be physically and emotionally cruel to children.

Munchausen Syndrome by proxy is rare, but women rather than men tend to display this psychological disturbance, which can be dangerous to the children involved (see page 11).

- Most sex abusers are male *but* most men do *not* sexually abuse children or young people. It is seriously unjust to develop a policy on early years employment that assumes all men are potential sex abusers.

Taken to extremes, this concern could mean that no men were allowed near children in any capacity. This exclusion would ban them as workers in early years centres, school and playwork facilities or as fathers with their own children. Such an extreme stance is unworkable and would seriously distort children's development. Human beings come in two sexes and boys and girls need both of them.

All early years centres need clear codes of conduct with children which apply to female as well as male workers. The inaccurate view that children are only at risk from male workers overlooks the capacity of some women to ill-treat children physically or emotionally. Paedophiles sometimes spend a considerable amount of time becoming accepted before they start to abuse children, so it is important that any code of conduct should apply to all workers, however long they have been involved with the centre, and whether they are paid for their work or give their time as a volunteer. Centres also need an atmosphere in which children, colleagues and parents feel able to voice any concerns promptly and with the confidence that someone will listen and take them seriously (see page 94).

EQUAL OPPORTUNITIES ISSUES

Discussion and argument in Britain has focused heavily on the inaccurate view that 'most abusers are men so . . .', but this is not the case in all countries. Publications from the European Commission Network on Childcare point out that countries in mainland Europe, especially in Scandinavia, have maintained equal opportunities by employing male workers. Child protection is a concern but is not assumed to be resolved by ensuring men do not work with young children. The following are strong reasons for employing both sexes in an early years team:

- Children need to relate to men *and* women who provide positive role models of being an adult.
- Putting equal opportunities on sex into practice ideally needs a mixed-sex team. It is far more effective for children to learn and play alongside male workers who show a gentle side, or are good cooks, than to tell children this is a possibility, or depend on books and posters.

- Workers may well have different styles because of their sex as well as their individual differences. As long as the roles of workers do not become stereotyped, or one sex corners all the interesting work, then children will experience different styles through contact with workers of both sexes.
- Children in some lone parent homes may not have much contact with a positive male figure. Children from homes disrupted by domestic violence may desperately need experience of a man who can be gentle, be patient and deal with conflict without violence.

Partnership with parents

Establishing a friendly working relationship with parents is part of good practice in an early years setting. You should be aiming for an effective partnership and exploring what this means for your centre, even if you never have any child protection concerns. An open and friendly relationship with parents can, however, make a substantial difference when concerns about abuse do arise.

Children need to experience positive role models of both sexes

Talking with Parents

Regular conversations with parents should be normal experience for them and will make them more comfortable about discussing a range of issues with you. Make sure that you exchange interesting and positive experiences of their child and let them know about any minor mishaps in the centre that have involved or hurt their child. You should also exchange information about their child's health, such as whether their child has developed a slight temperature at the end of the day or that there are two cases of chicken pox in the nursery. These kinds of conversation build a relationship which communicates your interest in their child, your wish to keep them informed and to listen to their views and information.

It is bad practice for workers to develop the habit of only talking to parents if there is a problem. The result of this imbalance is that parents will, not surprisingly, be wary as soon as you approach them. They will be ready to defend themselves or their child against criticism. If you then have a serious worry, parents are far less likely to listen and discuss it with you than if you have a friendly relationship. It will never be easy to have a conversation with a parent that arises because of an unexplained injury to the child or because

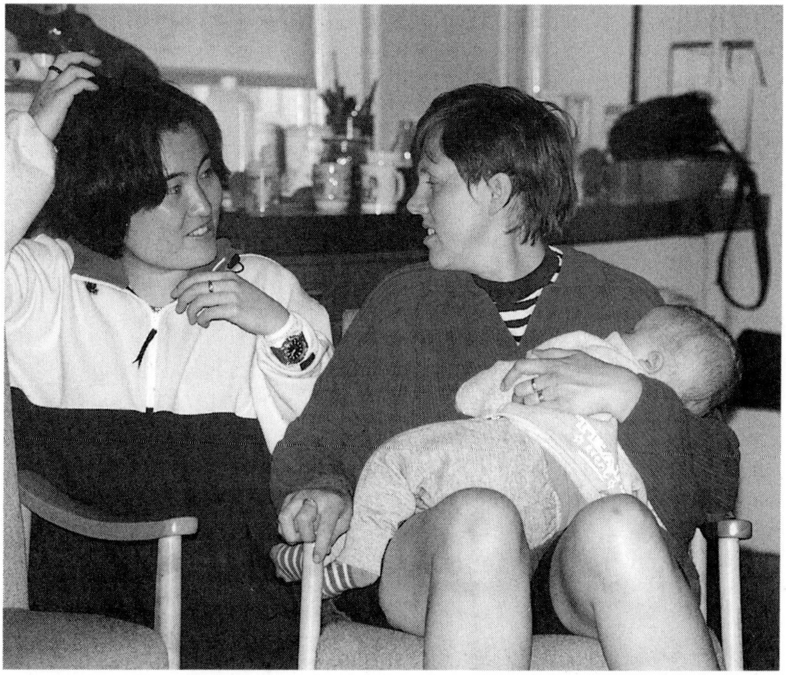

Establishing effective working relationships with parents

the child has made a worrying remark, but it will be easier if you have established yourself with the parents as somebody who cares about the children and is not always ready to criticise and blame parents.

Sometimes it will be a parent, or another carer of the child, who raises a worry with you. Again, parents are far more likely to approach you if they have developed confidence in you as someone who will listen and react appropriately. Most workers are concerned about the prospect of tackling parents about a worry, but overlook the possibility that parents may sometimes have worries themselves: about a member of their family, a neighbour or a centre worker or volunteer. Parents may find it difficult to approach a member of staff, however much they feel that they must say something.

ACTIVITY

Over a period of two weeks, keep track of all your conversations with parents, however short. Note down:

- The name of the parent with whom you spoke.
- The day and approximate time of the conversation.
- The topic of conversation and in brief what was said.

If it is possible, also keep a note of conversations when parents approach you.

Look back over your record afterwards and consider the following honestly:

1 Are there any parents with whom you rarely, if ever, speak? Are there some with whom it is usually only a very short exchange? What might be the possible reasons for this?
2 Can you see any imbalance in the reasons for which you start a conversation with parents, or with some parents in particular? Is it usually to raise problems with some, or many, of the parents?
3 What can you do to redress any imbalances? Talk over your findings with a colleague. Perhaps you all find it hard to approach certain parents. If this is the case, you need to discuss how to deal with it.

Access to Records

Parents should be informed that you keep an accident book of incidents in the centre and that they have access to any records about their own child. Some centres have space on records or a diary of a child so that parents can contribute their views, in agreement or disagreement. Parents will be less disturbed about any recording for child protection concerns if they can see this activity as part of the centre's good practice in keeping accurate and objective records. Centres which do not give parents easy access to their children's records are creating potential trouble. Parents may well assume that the records are biased or full of critical remarks about the children and parents.

In your setting it should be clear to parents, and to any professionals with whom you work:

- What records you keep on a regular basis.
- The reasons for keeping these records and details of children's development, to show that your aims in identifying and tracking problems are not all negative.
- Your obligations about discussing concerns and to whom you would show records under these circumstances.
- How you work to ensure that your records are factual and objective.

You will find more about record keeping on page 105.

Child Protection Policy and Parents

It would be overwhelming for parents who were new to your setting if they were given copies of every policy or set of procedures and left to read them. Parents need to be given the key points about how your setting operates and told that they are welcome to look in greater detail at any policies if they wish. The key points about child protection for parents are that:

- Staff at the centre have a commitment to children's health and development.
- Part of the work is an obligation to follow up concerns about any child's physical well-being, emotional state or behaviour.
- Usual practice is to discuss any worries first with the child's parent(s) or carer.
- If workers, or the parent(s), feel concerned that child protection is an issue, then the matter has to be referred to social services.
- The written records on children are open to those children's parent(s) or other permanent carer.

- If parents have any concerns about their child(ren) or about any member of staff, then they can raise them with a worker or the head of the centre, as they see fit.

These points might be drafted into a written leaflet but good communication includes spoken exchanges as well. It is important for workers to be able to explain the ideas informally in conversation in order to put parents at ease. Also, some parents may not be confident readers and may welcome a brief discussion as well as having a written leaflet to take away.

ACTIVITY

Using the key points suggested for communication with parents about child protection, compose a short leaflet for parents.

1 Discuss your wording with a colleague and consider any suitable revisions. You could also discuss the leaflet with a friend who is not involved in early years work. Such a person can often be a good judge of whether a leaflet is clear or is full of early years jargon.
2 Take the opportunity also to practise fielding likely questions about how the procedures work.

In many child protection cases children will stay in the early years setting that they have been attending. The exceptions are likely to be if children are taken into care because of the nature of the concerns, or if protection issues have arisen about the setting. Relationships with the parent(s) may not be easy (see page 126) but the day care or education arrangement for the child is more likely to continue if:

- There has been an open relationship established between workers and the parent(s).
- The parent(s) do not feel judged or accused by the worker and are confident that written records are accurate and do not include speculation.

Workers are often worried that a parent may be angry with the centre or individual workers. However, it is also possible that a parent is looking for support and trusts the worker to provide it. Some parents will seek help when they recognise that they are close to ill-treating their child. In some child protection cases, the parent with whom you are working will not be the suspected abuser (see Chapter 5).

Working with other professionals and agencies

WORKING WELL TOGETHER

Under the Children Act 1989, it is a legal requirement of all professionals to work co-operatively and involve all the relevant parties in a child protection case. Early years settings other than schools are, unfortunately, often left out of this process.

You may find that your local child protection team does value and understand the important role of early years centres. On the other hand, you may find an unchecked assumption, founded in a lack of knowledge of the kind of work that you do, that day care settings cannot contribute to child protection. For the sake of the children, it is important that early years settings do not wait to be approached but are ready to make the first contact if they are being left out of the process. Try to establish regular channels of communication before you have a crisis.

You can show other professionals that:

- You understand the process of child protection and your possible role in the system.
- Your position with the children and families gives you an insight into individual children and an opportunity to monitor worrying changes or problems.
- You employ good practice in keeping records and respect the appropriate boundaries to confidentiality and access.
- You respect their professional status and anticipate respect in turn.

YOUR LOCAL CHILD PROTECTION SYSTEM

You need to know your local network and have relevant names and contact numbers easily to hand. No early years centre should wait for a crisis before finding out who they should contact about a child protection concern. An early years worker would normally speak with his/her head of centre in the first instance and the head would then contact the person responsible for child protection locally. This might be one of several people and your local guidelines should make this clear. The possibilities are outlined below.

Chapter 2 describes the child protection system as a whole but there are slight differences between areas. Every centre should have a file that includes the following items of information:

- The person who is responsible for your centre under the Children Act obligations of registration and inspection. S/he may be called a Day Care Advisor or an Under-Eights Inspector or some other combination of these terms. This person may be your first point of contact if you have a concern. S/he could also be a good place to start if you are investigating how the child protection system works locally.
- Every local authority has an Emergency Social Work Duty Team, but these may be different for different areas of a large local authority. You need this telephone number in your file or pinned to the centre office board with other important contact numbers. It may be possible within normal working hours to reach the Duty Social Worker in the Child and Family Team for your area.
- Your area may have a specialist Child Protection Team or a Co-ordinator. This person would also be a good place to start in understanding how child protection works in your area. The co-ordinator should be able to advise you about training courses or workshops that will help members of the centre team to understand child protection.
- The NSPCC has a legal right to start or to investigate child protection issues. Inquiries to the national head office are referred to the local social services or to the local NSPCC team if appropriate.
- Your local police should have an individual or a team responsible for child protection concerns. They may go under the name of Child Protection or Family Protection Unit or Team. You should know that they exist and their contact number.

You should know exactly how the child protection system works in your area before there is a crisis.

- You should know whom to contact first when the head of centre decides that there is a child protection issue about a child.
- You should know whom you should call if this person is not available.
- It is unlikely that the police would be your first contact. The exception would be if a parent, or other carer, were attacking a child within your centre and their behaviour was so aggressive that it was unsafe for staff to intervene. You should then call the police as you would for any incident where safety was a serious concern.

YOUR LOCAL NETWORK

Some early years settings work in an isolated way, either because they are geographically a long way from other centres or because different types of early years settings are not in contact with each other. There are advantages to an active early years network: workers can support each other, discussions on different topics can be useful and setting up workshops may be more feasible if several centres are interested. An active network can also support you in finding out about child protection locally. Senior workers can also make sure that all the early years centres present a positive and professional image to child protection specialists who do not initially think to involve them.

If you would like to find out more about creating your own local network you could try the following:

- Find out if there are any local early years forums. The National Early Years Network (see page 180 for address) has been active in promoting the development of forums.
- National organisations may help in making links with centres who share your focus, whether they are close to you or not (see the list of useful addresses for some suggestions).
- Consider making direct contact with other early years settings close to you, whether or not they are the same kind of centre. Some private nurseries can find that they are in competition with each other when there are more places locally than children to fill them, yet a sharing of ideas and policies on child protection will benefit everyone.

Raising the Profile of Early Years Settings

Generally speaking local child protection guidelines are more likely to involve schools in the process and to overlook the importance of early years centres and their work. Areas vary and you may find that your local child protection team appreciates the important role of nurseries, playgroups and other centres, or you may find that your kind of centre scarcely rates a mention in the local guidelines. If this is the case and you are a senior worker, you need to take steps to show what your team can do as part of professional inter-agency work.

- Be ready to make the move towards the local child protection team rather than sitting back and thinking 'They ought to contact us!'
- Set up regular channels of communication so that you have established professional links before there is a child protection concern or crisis.
- Show that you understand how the child protection process works, the ways in which your centre could contribute and that you are clear about what your centre should leave to other professionals within the process.
- Develop and maintain appropriate policies and procedures and let the child protection team know what you do and how.

- Show that you understand good practice in record keeping, appropriate confidentiality and passing on of information, and in developing a professional working relationship with parents.
- Prepare thoroughly for any meetings, such as informal ones with a social worker, or case conferences (if you are invited to attend). Organise in advance the information you have to contribute and the facts underpinning any opinions that are expressed. You will have to be confident in presenting the perspective and observations of your centre. It is pointless to complain afterwards that nobody asked you; you have to be ready to speak up, if necessary.
- The head of centre and any senior workers are responsible for ensuring that good practice is maintained in the centre and for coaching, supporting and organising training for staff. Good practice in the centre requires an atmosphere in which workers feel able to ask for help or a second opinion and are encouraged to learn from new experiences.

You will find more about working with other professionals on page 111.

Anti-discriminatory practice

What is normal in families?

All early years workers need a broad base of knowledge to make sensible and properly supported judgements. 'Normal' is certainly not just what you know from your own childhood or of families whom you knew then, or know personally now. Every worker, whatever their personal cultural and ethnic background, has to make the effort to extend his/her knowledge of family traditions and ways of raising children.

An awareness of different cultures and approaches to children has to be part of a more general awareness that adults vary in how they deal with children and in what they feel is appropriate behaviour from adults towards children. Some parents may be less demonstrative than you in your dealings with children. Less overt affection does not necessarily mean that an adult cares less about a child; people have different ways of showing that they care. Alternatively, you may feel that some parents are too emotional with their children. None of these differences may relate to cultural traditions but are linked instead to particular families and their personal style. However, if you do not share a culture with a parent or know that you differ in religious beliefs, it is easy to assume that the different patterns arise from broader cultural differences. This explanation may or may not be valid.

Differences Within a Culture

Opinions about the right way to raise children change over time and can be very different between different social classes within the same culture. For instance, there has been considerable criticism of women who are working mothers and who use day care facilities, but there has never been a similar criticism of wealthy families who delegate the majority of child care to the family nanny followed by boarding school.

In Britain there are striking differences of opinion between people of a very similar cultural background about the acceptability of physical forms of discipline with children. Some adults, parents and professionals are strongly opposed to hitting children or any other kind of physical punishment. An equally strong lobby is in favour of hitting young children on the grounds that it is all they understand in some circumstances and that denying this option to adults will lead to badly behaved children (see page 160).

Differences Between Cultures

Cultural tradition can be a strong influence on how parents raise their children, react towards sons and daughters and resolve matters of authority in the family.

It is regarded as normal in Britain that mothers take the primary responsibility for children, although there is more variation in this pattern now than a couple of generations ago. But in some cultures, for instance some African and African-Caribbean cultures, it is much more usual for the care of children to be shared between relatives, who are probably female. It is also accepted that parents leave some or all of their children with the extended family while they go elsewhere in search of work, sometimes a considerable distance. This pattern is borne out by some West African families in England who have sought long-term private fostering for their children while they worked or completed studies.

So, it is unacceptable for a worker to criticise a shared care family system on the grounds that 'it should be the mother'. On the other hand, the system must work for the safety and well-being of the child. A shared care system can fail children just as some mothers in sole charge have abused or neglected their children. Any professional involved with the families should still be concerned about the quality of care for children in the extended family or any private fostering arrangements, but delegating responsibility for the child care has to be seen in the context of cultural tradition.

Issues in child protection

Anti-discriminatory practice is part of general good practice in early years work, but particular issues and dilemmas can arise in child protection.

Assumptions and Beliefs

Your approach to child protection concerns should include an awareness of your feelings and assumptions, just like any other aspect of your practice.

- In child protection it is important that you do not assume that particular kinds of families are more, or less, likely to abuse or neglect their children. You should take each child and their family as individuals and, if you have concerns, make sure that you have a sound basis for deciding there is a possible child protection worry.
- Consult with colleagues and with your head of centre. They should support you in standing back from a family and talking through what has happened and why you are worried.
- You might want to check that you are not more ready to suspect abuse or neglect because your relationship with the parent has never been easy or because you disapprove of their approach to discipline.
- On the other hand, you might need just as much support and a chance to talk when you are tempted to think, 'This is such a nice family, surely they couldn't harm their child?'
- It is racist to assume that families of a particular cultural or religious background are more likely to abuse or neglect their children. These views must be dealt with firmly by a senior worker or head of centre. The attitude is prejudiced, regardless of the worker's background and that of the families.
- On the other hand, workers need support in exploring their concerns when they do not share a cultural or religious identity with the family. Staff may be so concerned that they might be thought racist, or in some other way prejudiced, that they may not voice concerns that should be checked.
- Any kind of assumptions about a family need to be checked, and possibly challenged, in a positive way, through discussion in your centre and through the supervision process. A worker might assume that a lone parent will be without any family back-up but some lone parents have a very effective network of family and friends. In contrast, perhaps another worker assumes, without asking, that the struggling Indian mother will be fine 'because all Asians live in an extended family, don't they?' But this mother may be on her own without any family support.
- Language and understanding can be an issue in sensitive conversations, even when worker and parent share the same language. People use

their words, expressiveness in their tone of voice and all the accompanying body language in varied ways. Differences of culture and social class are often reflected in what is said and how, especially if emotions become involved.

- If you do not share a language with a parent then you need to know who is the parent's preferred interpreter. This choice is another issue that needs to have been resolved early in the relationship, before you face a difficult conversation.

The key point is that assumptions can be misleading and may put children at risk. Unchecked assumptions might be prejudiced, but are not inevitably so. You need to be ready to ask yourself, or accept questions from colleagues such as 'What is my basis for assuming this?' and 'What makes me so sure?' Senior workers are very important in guiding the team through delicate issues such as these.

Knowledge

You need to take account of different ways of raising children. It is not justified to assume that the way you were brought up, or the way that you and your colleagues deal with children, is the only right way. You need to

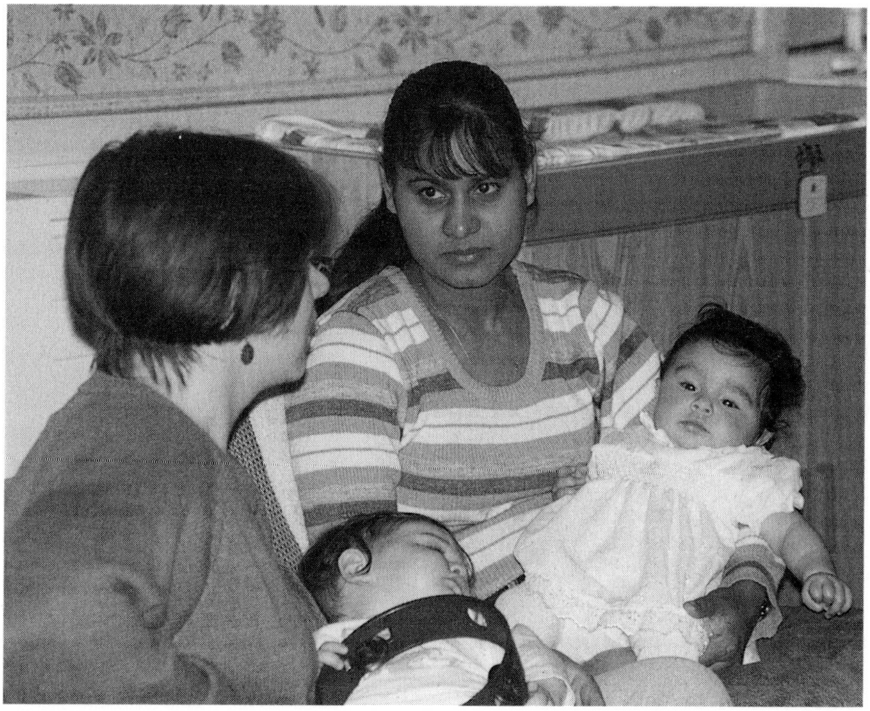

Learning about different cultures from each other

be open to other possibilities and this should be your approach, whatever your own cultural or religious background.

It is good practice to be ready to learn more about different cultures and beliefs but you need to gain a broad base of knowledge. You can use several different approaches:

- Learn from other people by talking, asking questions and listening to colleagues, parents and friends who have different experience and knowledge. However, do not expect everyone to be an expert and handle your questioning with sensitivity. Imagine how might you feel if you were asked searching questions such as 'Is this really normal in your culture?' or 'Does everybody do this with their children?'
- Learn from reading and by watching relevant television programmes.
- Take advantage of training courses and workshops.

ACTIVITY

The main aim in learning more about cultures other than your own is to develop general knowledge, so that you have a reasonable basis for understanding to what extent a family is following a cultural or religious tradition and how much is purely family style. Obviously, the two overlap in many families.

Think carefully about three or four families whom you know well and who share your own cultural background. These may be families you know through work but think also about one or two families whom you know through personal contact.

1. If someone from a very different cultural background met each of these families, how far do you judge s/he could take them as representative of your culture? Would you tend to say, 'In some ways, yes, but in some ways, no?' If so, in what ways are these families 'typical' or 'untypical'?
2. Do you feel it would be misleading to generalise from these families without further experience? What could this tell you about the risks when early years workers feel they know a particular culture or a religion from contact with a small number of families?

BE CAREFUL OF GENERALISATIONS

Knowing one or two examples of families from a particular cultural, national or religious background is not a safe basis for assuming that you know all there is to know about this group. If you met a few families from Devon, you could not assume that you were well informed about family life in the West Country, let alone the rest of England or Britain. Yet people do sometimes think that contact with a couple of Indian families somehow informs them about Indian traditions as a whole, not accounting for the tremendous diversity in culture, religion and social status that actually exists within the large Indian population of Britain.

You should also be careful not to make assumptions about any culture from working with families who are under stress. Families experiencing stress or crisis are not usually behaving in a way that might be termed 'normal' for them in calmer times, let alone typical of the culture or religion to which they belong.

EVERYONE NEEDS TO LEARN

It is poor practice to assume that any black worker will somehow understand and be the best person to work with any black family loosely defined. The worker may well have empathy with others who have experienced ill treatment as a result of racism, but this possibly shared experience does not provide detailed knowledge about another person's culture.

Early years settings should avoid any crude racial matching of workers to families, or parents, when there is a delicate issue to broach. Black workers will not necessarily be in tune with every black family, any more than white workers will be in agreement with any given white family. Why on earth should they be? The terms 'black' and 'white' cover a tremendous variety of individual people and cultural backgrounds.

So, unless s/he has specific experience and knowledge, a worker of African-Caribbean origin, for example, will not be any better equipped than a white worker to relate to a Somali refugee family, a Mandarin-speaking Chinese family or a family from Bengal. It is important that senior workers remember this and you must voice your concerns if you are expected to have unrealistic levels of knowledge on the basis of your own culture, religion or skin colour.

Challenging cultural traditions

Checking your assumptions about a particular family is harder when you do not know the culture very well. Among many other tough questions, you are also asking yourself whether you are observing a cultural tradition that you have misunderstood. However, ill-treatment of children cannot be excused by assuming, or even concluding on the basis of good information, that the parents' actions are led by cultural tradition or by deeply held religious beliefs.

Anti-discriminatory practice in child protection has to hold a delicate balance. You should not reject other ways of child rearing because it is not your culture's way, but equally a practice is not made acceptable because it is associated with a long cultural tradition. No individual worker should try to weigh up such complex issues on her/his own. It is sensible and professional to consult your head of centre or the other people involved in the child protection system (listed on page 69).

Children from a wide variety of different cultural backgrounds can and have been damaged by their family's actions or inaction. Whatever the strength of a cultural tradition or a religious belief, you must ask the same questions when you weigh up what any individual parent is doing or not doing with regard to a child. Bear in mind that in a child protection case it will not be the responsibility of the early years setting to come to conclusions about abuse. However, you will be able to pass on to the child protection team your concerns and desire to understand the possible impact of the family's culture or religious beliefs on what is happening.

- Questions have to be asked, such as, 'What is the impact of this practice on the child?' or 'What is the experience of the children in this family?'
- No cultural tradition or religious belief should result in harm to a child or endanger his/her health. For example, parents' strongly held views about physical punishment do not excuse injuries to their child. See also the discussion about female circumcision on pages 12–13.
- Even when you are uncertain about a family's cultural traditions you should never overlook visible physical injury to a child. Be wary when a child's explanation of the injury does not match what his/her parents are saying, or when other records that you keep raise independent concerns about this child's health or development.
- It can be hard to put your own strongly held beliefs to one side when a family's approach is very different to your own. But you can be

objective, and not swayed by assumptions, when you follow good practice in record keeping in your centre (see page 105). Make sure that you are up to date with children's development and their patterns of behaviour. Good observation skills and assessment will help you to focus on the child: regardless of what seem to be the parents' child rearing practices, you will be able to ascertain how the child is progressing.

- A balanced overview of a child's well-being and any child protection issues has to include a cultural perspective, but all workers need to be on their guard against an uncritical acceptance of a family's way because it is assumed to be, or definitely is, based in cultural or religious traditions.

Case studies

You can use the following examples to explore some of the issues raised in this chapter and to stimulate discussion about your own practice and that of the early years setting of which you have most experience. You can think over the examples and make notes for yourself but, ideally, use some in discussion with colleagues or fellow-students. For each case study you should ask:

- What are the main issues in this situation?
- What is unclear from the information so far? What other information might you need to know in order to understand better what seems to be happening?
- What would be a sensible first step if you were facing this situation?

You might want to return to some of the examples when you have read Chapters 4 and 5.

NATASHA

Natasha is four years old and her family came to England from Jamaica when her mother was still a child. Natasha lives with her mother and two aunts and other relatives live within two streets of her home. You have become increasingly concerned because neither you, nor Natasha, ever knows who will pick her up from nursery school and some days it is up to half an hour after the end of the session before anyone arrives. Natasha always recognises the person and seems content to go but has said to you, 'I wish Mummy or Auntie Tess would pick me up.'

This week the arrangements for Natasha have become even less predictable. On two mornings you found her in the nursery front yard when you came to work, an hour before any child should arrive. You spoke with the aunt who arrived in the afternoon and were told, 'I can't help it. I have to get to work and you're here anyway aren't you?'

In the middle of the week, the nursery's handyman struck up a conversation with you about Natasha. 'They live two doors down from us. Poor little sod, nobody watches out for her. One evening she was wandering on the pavement in her nightie until one of them shouted out of the window at her. She wants to come in and play with our two and that's fine by the wife. So, she phones up and half the time Natasha's Mum doesn't even know she's gone and the aunties think my wife's odd for calling anyway. These people don't know how to look after kids properly. Now *my* wife is home with ours . . .'

Aaron

Aaron is three years old and has been in the playgroup for two months. On his left hand, he has an extra finger, which is floppy and does not work like a finger. Aaron does not seem to be too worried and his mother has explained that they are waiting for surgery to deal with the problem. You have noticed that a new worker seems to avoid being close to Aaron and has visibly shuddered when she looked at the boy's left hand. In the garden you noticed her ignore Aaron's outstretched hand as he asked to be helped down from the climbing frame. Today, you overheard this worker say to a parent, 'It's horrible. That floppy thing gives me the creeps.'

Ann-Marie

Ann-Marie has attended your nursery for nearly three months. Her parents are fundamentalist Christians, who were initially doubtful about the nursery's behaviour policy. Her father especially made a strong case that children needed firmer discipline than the nursery appeared to provide. Ann-Marie came in last week with severe bruising to her bottom, which became obvious because she winced when she sat at the table to play. When you asked her father about the bruises, he was evasive, saying, 'You wouldn't understand. Children need guidance and Ann-Marie is very wilful.'

Ann-Marie did not return to the nursery for three days by which time she no longer seemed to be in pain. Today you notice red welts on Ann-Marie's palms and she is unwilling to explain what has happened beyond saying that she was 'very naughty'. At pick-up time Ann-Marie's mother is initially apologetic about an unspecified 'accident' to her daughter. Then she blurts out, 'Anyway my husband says you should respect our beliefs and what we do in our own home. We've got a copy of your equal opportunities statement. Respect us then!' And she rushes off with Ann-Marie.

Greg

You have been hearing an increased amount of noise from the room next to the one where you work with your group of children. A student on work placement appears to have taken a dislike to one of the children. She always calls him 'Gregory O'Connor', although he is known as Greg to everyone else and children in the centre are not usually addressed by their first and family name. Over the last week most of her shouting appears to have been aimed at Greg and you thought you heard her say, 'Dumb Irish tinkers'.

Your colleague next door has been showing the student how to complete the centre's developmental records on children. As you passed the door of that room you saw the student propel Greg into a chair and say, 'Right, Gregory O'Connor. Let's see all the things you can't do.' Matters come to a head when you are in the room briefly as lunch is being served and are chatting with Greg. The student ignores you, leans over to Greg and shouts very close to his ear, 'You shut up, Gregory O'Connor! No talking at mealtimes!' You say to the student, 'I was talking with Greg' and she just stares at you.

4

Child Protection in Early Years Settings

Part of your role in the whole process of child protection will be the work that goes on within your early years setting. This chapter focuses on what you can do, and includes some reminders of what you should not attempt, within your own centre. Undoubtedly, the pattern of work will be different, depending on your position in the centre. The role of a head of centre or senior worker is different from that of a key or family worker or assistant, but all roles are important.

There is a considerable amount that you can do, usefully and properly, in an early years setting when possible child protection concerns arise. You can listen, talk and make sense of what has emerged through the broad base of knowledge and observation in the setting. What you definitely do *not* do, however senior your position, is to start a formal investigation relating to child protection.

When you have concerns

Keeping a perspective on child abuse

Child abuse is a serious issue and has strong emotional overtones for anyone who cares about the well-being of children. Early years workers who are coming to terms with the possibility of abuse need support, usually from senior workers, to maintain a realistic perspective on the situation.

'It Couldn't Happen Here'

It is sometimes easier to assume that child abuse is a problem that happens elsewhere. Yet it is important that early years workers allow for the possibility that child protection issues could arise in their setting – wherever they work and whatever the range of families whose children attend.

You may be reluctant to consider child abuse because you cannot believe that a parent, or a colleague, could possibly ill-treat a child. Of course, you should neither suspect nor condemn out of hand, but neither should you push aside concerns because of an inaccurate image of the kind of person who would abuse children. You may also be worried about being wrong. It is responsible of you to allow for doubts, but it would be against the children's interests if those doubts led you to do nothing. Your centre's procedures (see page 53) should be clear on what steps to take and whom you should consult.

Doubts and worries are natural, as are concerns about making unsupported accusations of anyone, but children will be placed at risk if you allow such doubts to stop you voicing a concern about a child. Nor can you assume that someone else will notice and speak up; perhaps nobody else will notice, or perhaps you are the only person whom this child has told about his/her experience. You are not having such doubts just because you are an early years worker; other professionals also have to deal with these feelings. Social workers must follow clear procedures because even specialist training in child protection does not allow them to act as they personally see fit.

'Child Abuse is Everywhere'

Chapter 1 included a detailed discussion of warning signs of different kinds of child abuse that should alert you to the need to explore further. It is important to take your own concerns, or those expressed by children and parents, with seriousness, but it is also good practice to exercise some caution and not to leap to conclusions.

It is good practice to recognise that you need to take some further steps, but poor practice to decide swiftly that you are definitely dealing with a case of child abuse.

- There can often be more than one possible explanation for an incident that concerns you or for something worrying about a child's behaviour or development. A troublesome, anxious or developmentally delayed child may be experiencing stress, which may or may not be due to abuse. Some action may need to be taken, including a careful discussion with the parents, but it is not necessarily a case for child protection.
- There are no quick and easy checklists for child abuse. Some practical leaflets describe worrying signs in brief but you need to remember that careful observation and discussion will raise a number of 'ifs' and 'buts'. You are usually looking for patterns rather than single incidents. Be very wary of any booklets that claim to be providing definitive signs of abuse.

- Especially remember that worrying signs are not a simple two-way street. Some children who wet the bed are reacting to the distress of being abused, but *not* all bedwetters have experienced abuse.
- It is important that early years teams do not dismiss the possibility of child abuse out of hand, with the claim that 'We don't have those kinds of families here' or that 'No worker would ever behave like that, so the child must be mistaken.' Yet a team must not become so concerned about the likelihood of abuse, of any kind, that all problems or accidents are believed to be caused by child abuse.

If you are a senior worker, your role will be to help your team remain alert to the signs of child abuse but also to keep the issues in perspective: most children are not abused. You will be in a different position if your centre specialises in working with families under stress or if your referral system is designed to respond to concerns about families.

The source of your concerns

There are several different ways in which you may be alerted to the possible abuse of a child in your care:

- You notice something that makes you worry – either a particular incident or the pattern emerging from your observations and records of a child.
- The child says something, does something, or his/her behaviour has changed in a way that catches your attention.
- A child's parents may confide in you – something about themselves or their concerns about another person involved in family life, or a member of your own team.
- Someone else approaches you with their concerns – another professional or a non-family member, such as a friend or neighbour.

Through your own thinking, discussion with a colleague or your senior and then through appropriate recording, you need to ascertain:

- What exactly is concerning you and your reasons for concern. You need to reach a specific description.
- Why your observations or what you have been told are a source of concern; why it matters.
- Or, what the reasons are for not being seriously concerned about an incident that has occurred.

Your observations

Observing Children

Good practice is to keep accurate and descriptive records of children's development, interests and behaviour. These records are invaluable in keeping track of children's progress, identifying areas in which you can offer a child positive help and in sharing information with parents. The main reason for setting up records and for observing children is to monitor their learning and general well-being and the effectiveness of your provision for them – not to carry out a child protection check. However, good quality records of individual children and your own alert observations can highlight patterns that you should be ready to explore further, such as a child who used to play with interest and enthusiasm becoming quiet and very withdrawn, or another seeming generally unwell, with cuts and bruises that take a long time to heal.

Your developmental records could be very important in assessing concerns about a child. Certainly, some reviews of practice in child protection have stressed the importance of keeping a detailed account of how a child is progressing and behaving on a daily basis (see page 48).

Observing Parents or Other Carers

Most early years workers will not be making formal observations of parents or other carers of the children. The possible exception will be if you work in a specialist family or children's centre, where your contract with the parents requires that they attend as well as their children.

Informal observations of parents and conversations will help to build a fuller picture of the child. Children often behave differently with their families than they do in an early years centre, because the two settings are different. Partnership with parents is part of good practice and within this framework it is important to have conversations with parents about their children or what is happening in the centre. These discussions should be taking place as normal daily events, whether or not there are problems (see page 64).

However, your communication with parents and your observations of them with their children in the centre may give rise to concerns that should be explored. Some possibilities are that:

- You are concerned that these parents rarely speak positively of their child. Their approach does not seem to be one of modesty about their child but rejection by word and action. You have never heard them praise their child and they criticise him/her as a matter of course.

- These parents have very high expectations for their child, which seem to you to be inappropriate for his/her age. The demanding expectations are linked with criticism of the child for failing to meet the family's standards.
- In a family where there are several carers of the child you become concerned that nobody seems to be keeping an eye on what is happening to the child. Each carer seems to think that someone else is dealing with an issue. You are now worried that the child's health or development problem is falling through the net.
- A parent handles his/her child roughly in the centre – pushing and shoving him/her into his/her coat on a regular basis. She has also been seen to drag him/her along with such speed on the nursery path that the child fell over.

You need to be aware, especially if you yourself are not a parent, that all parents have times when they are not as thoughtful as they should be towards their children. You are looking at a pattern and assessing whether the harsh words are usual, or if this week has been particularly stressful in the family. Some parents are considerably harder on their children if there is an audience, especially of people whom the parent thinks might judge them negatively.

When children say something

Sometimes, your first source of concern will be what a child says to you. The child may confide in you about something that is happening at home or the actions of someone in particular. Alternatively, an important confidence may follow from a question you ask, such as 'That's a big bump on your forehead, David. How did that happen?' The following guidelines will help you when a child confides in you. This pattern is appropriate whatever the confidence the child is sharing, but the approach can be especially important if the child's words raise the issue of abuse.

Listen

The most important thing you can do is to *listen* to what the child is telling you. Good listening should be a skill that you continue to develop in all your other work with children and it is the most valuable when a child starts to confide in you.

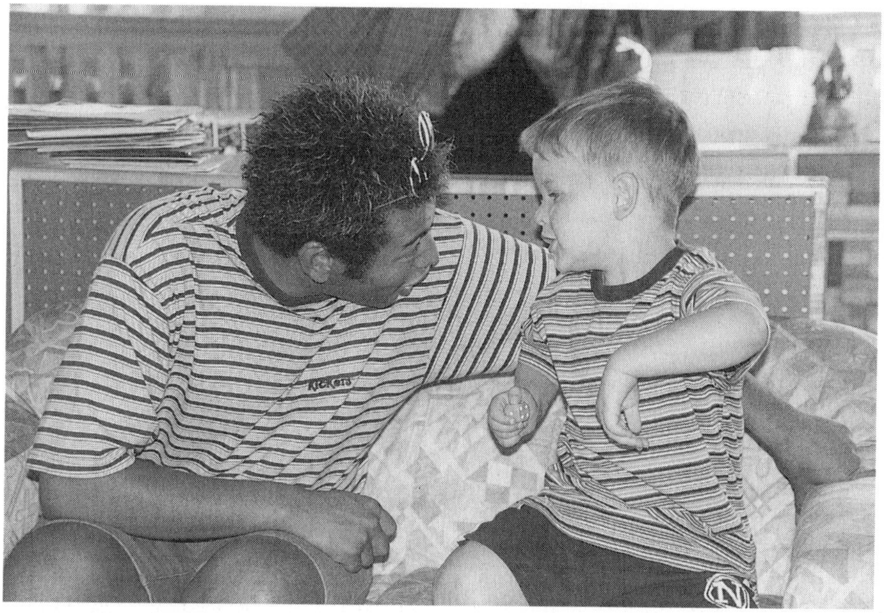

Sometimes children confide in you

- Give the child your full attention and listen to his/her words. This moment may not be the most convenient for you, but recognise that it is the moment that this child has become able to tell you something that matters to him/her.
- Hear the words s/he is using and the way s/he tells you this confidence. Watch him/her so that you can also 'hear' what s/he tells you through his/her body language.
- Be guided by the child and do not press him/her to talk for longer than s/he wants or to answer lots of questions.
- Do not stop a child who is talking freely to you in order to bring in a colleague, either a more senior worker or someone else, because you feel you need a witness to the conversation. This action is inappropriate and will probably stop the child talking.
- A child may choose a time when s/he can speak to you without being overheard. If other children come to get your attention you can courteously ask them to wait with, 'I'll be with you shortly, Andrea wants to have a word with me' or 'Can you just let Delroy and me talk in private for a while.'

It is important that the whole team within any early years setting is confident to listen in this way to a disclosure from a child. It is the job of the head of centre and other senior workers to make sure that all staff understand that good quality communication skills are needed, and not some additional, specific skills which only apply to child protection. Children will not be helped if less senior staff feel that they have to stop such a conversation and effectively refer a child on to a more senior member of staff.

Use open-ended questions

An appropriate and supportive conversation for a child is one in which the adult follows his/her lead and stops when the child wishes.

- Keep any questions you ask open-ended, and do not push a child in specific directions.
- Depending on what the child tells you, you might ask the kind of encouraging question that is part repetition of what a child has just said or a comment left unfinished. For instance, perhaps a child says, 'My big cousin is nasty to me' and you could follow up with, 'Nasty in what way, Sandy?' or a similar phrase. A child might whisper, 'Somebody hurt me' and, if you ask quietly, 'You say somebody hurt you?', you may not even have to ask the more specific question, 'Who hurt you, Daria?' This kind of gentle questioning is sometimes called **reflective listening**.
- Depending on the flow of the conversation, other open-ended questions might be, 'You say you were frightened?' or 'What has happened to make you cry?' You can also simply encourage a child by your open and attentive expression and simple questions like 'Yes?' or 'Anything else you want to tell me?'
- Listen to what the child says about how s/he is feeling: 'I'm cross with him', 'She makes me cry and she doesn't care' or 'He says I'm a bad girl, that nobody will like me anymore.' Show empathy and support for the child: 'You're feeling cross now?' or 'I will always like you, Mario. Tell me what has happened.' Avoid telling the child how s/he is feeling or making guesses about his/her emotional state.
- Children who have been sexually abused by a known and liked person can be very emotionally confused. What would otherwise be proper expressions of affection have become distorted by inappropriate sexual contact. A child's sense of pleasure at the affection may be struggling with half-understood feelings that the physical form of expression was not right. As you listen, you may be feeling anger, shock or distress, but you cannot assume that the child necessarily shares your emotions. S/he may feel all of these and more, but you can only find out by listening to him/her.

It is important to avoid cross-questioning children since a series of questions can direct a delicate conversation in an unhelpful way.

- You do not know exactly what has happened or how the child feels about the experience or worry. Leading questions tend to be guided by your guesses or unsupported suspicions ('Did Daddy do this to you?') and risk distorting the communication.
- Children are suggestible and they may start to say what you appear to want to hear. It is your responsibility to hear what children want to tell you, in the way that they want to tell it. You need not feel responsible for gathering loads of information. If something worrying has occurred, then there will be opportunity for exploring in more detail later, probably led by a social worker.
- Asking lots of questions may also pressure children to give you more details than they wish at the time. Children, especially those in distress, may also agree to specific questions just to stop a persistent adult questioner and end the conversation. Some child protection inquiries have criticised social workers for persistent and directive questioning of children. So, this aspect of good communication is something that everyone should keep in mind.

Support and reassure

Children who disclose worrying secrets need reassurance from adults but you should not give any promises that you cannot keep.

- You should show your support and affirmation of the child by listening and following the child's lead in the conversation.
- Sometimes, you should give specific reassurance, such as, 'This isn't your fault', 'No, I'm not cross with you at all. I'm so glad you told me what's happening' or 'Of course I still like you and I want to help you with this.'
- It is not up to you to criticise the person who has hurt the child. In some cases of child abuse, the abuser is a loved relative and the turmoil of mixed emotions is part of the whole problem for children. You can still reassure the child with more general support such as, 'Kitty, nobody should make you this upset' rather than laying blame with, 'Your Grandad is a bad person.'
- Avoid questions like 'Why didn't you tell me before?', because this implies that you are disappointed with rather than concerned for the child. The reasons why a child has not disclosed until now may emerge but, for the moment, his/her reticence is less important than the fact

that s/he has now told you. 'Why?' questions will almost certainly put the child on the spot and are unhelpful – avoid them.

- You cannot promise a child that you will keep serious disclosures a secret. You have a responsibility to take such concerns further. Your next step might be to talk with a more senior worker, with the child's parent or to consult with someone else. Explain to the child, in words appropriate to his/her age and understanding, what you are going to do next.
- You cannot promise children that someone who has hurt or abused them will necessarily be punished – whether within the family or by law. You can promise that you will take the matter further and see what can be done and that you will listen to the child when s/he wants your time again.

ACTIVITY

You may find it useful to recall a time when you wanted to tell somebody about an experience of emotional importance to you. This memory need not necessarily be something from your childhood, but could be from your adult life.

1. How did the conversation go with the person in whom you confided? Did they listen to you? What made you feel that they were really listening?
2. What kind of comments did the other person make? What was helpful to you? What made you feel unsupported?
3. Did they ask you any questions? What kind of questions were helpful and which were not?
4. Did they ask, what seemed to you, too many questions? How did you feel on the receiving end of lots of questions?
5. Looking back over the conversation that you experienced, what lessons have you learned that can be applied to delicate conversations with children?

If possible, share some of your general thoughts with colleagues or fellow-students in a college group. Be considerate of each other as you discuss these issues. If your colleagues are sharing a difficult experience with the group, they will not want to be criticised or cross-questioned now about their memories and feelings.

Consult and make notes

Children, young or old, should not have to repeat a conversation to a whole series of adults in your setting after that first disclosure. When a child has confided in you, you need to consult a more senior worker who will help you to identify the most appropriate course of action. As the person in whom the child confided, you are responsible for making notes on the conversation as soon as possible, and certainly with no more delay than later in the same day. Your notes should include specific details of the conversation:

- When and where did the child talk to you? Were you alone with the child? Were any other staff or children within hearing? Did anyone else contribute to the conversation?
- What did the child say to you (as accurately as you can recall)? Do not note down actual words in inverted commas ('. . .') unless you are certain that those are definitely the child's own phrases.
- Your impressions and opinions will be valuable because you know this child, but support them with your reasons, for instance, 'I believe Sandy is very upset. When he said to me "My big cousin is nasty to me", Sandy was twisting his hair around one finger – the way he does when he is really distressed.'
- Do not add guesses or speculations to the written report – about the child's feelings, likely abusers or judgements about the possible truth of what the child has said. Keep your report factual and opinions supported with reasons and/or evidence.

Notes of this kind follow more general good practice in keeping accurate written reports; an accurate and descriptive record will be just as important if the concern turns out to have an explanation which is not worrying. A careful approach, taking into account what you know and what you do not, can support you in a delicate conversation with a parent that might start with 'I was worried/confused/taken aback by something that Tanya said to me today . . .' If there becomes reason for serious concern and steps are taken in a child protection investigation by social workers, then a responsible and specific first record will be important for any future work.

But is it true?

One of the major steps forward for children in child protection has been that what children say is now given more weight. The prevailing assumption of previous generations was that the word of a child was unreliable, especially if set against that of an adult. Children, especially young children, were assumed to confuse fact and fantasy and be prone to lying.

In child protection there has been a significant shift to a working assumption that what a child says is true. However, there are several subtle issues to consider in this aspect of good practice. These issues are laid out one by one below. It is worth reading this section more than once and discussing the points with colleagues because, although it is important to listen to children, it is not good practice to assume that *everything* they say is literally true. You would not make this assumption in other aspects of your practice and it is not appropriate in child protection.

- Your responsibility is to *take seriously* what the child is saying to you. You should show this seriousness and your respect for the child by following the guidelines for active listening given earlier (page 88).
- Adults should not doubt or dismiss what a child says just because it seems unlikely, the adult mentioned seems so nice or even because the child has been known to embroider the truth on other occasions.
- It is equally important not to turn the previously disrespectful attitudes towards children on their head and take the child's perspective as the absolute truth without any more exploration. People sometimes promote an over-simple line of 'Believe the children; children never lie about abuse'. There needed to be a reaction to tendencies to disbelieve children, but the situation is more complex than this statement implies.
- Children, just like adults, have their own perspectives. They are giving you their view of events, which you should respect and take seriously. But there is a big difference between taking further the concern of 'Delia told me that her baby-sitter shows her "naughty pictures" ' and that of 'Delia's baby-sitter is definitely abusing her.'
- It is very unlikely that children will lie about abuse. They are far more likely to have difficulty in telling you, especially if the person harming them is a member of their family or someone the child knows is liked and respected. But it is possible that a child may say only part of what is happening or will only be able to express a fraction of their distress. So, the assumption that the child has told you the whole truth in one conversation could be a harmful conclusion to draw. Perhaps the child has told you only what she has managed to get out this time and there is more to tell.
- Although it is unlikely that children will lie about abuse, there have been cases when children have become entangled in adults' bitter relationships and what the children have said has reflected what an

adult has wanted to believe. There have been legal cases where children, usually older ones, have been badgered by one parent into false accusations against another, as part of vicious custody disputes.

In summary, children's disclosures to you should be given the same respect as the worrying confidences of any adult. What they say should be taken seriously, but not fixed as the whole truth that will override anything that anyone else says, or as the final facts of the case.

What stops children telling?

Children do not always speak up about abuse and there are a number of reasons why they may not tell, or may not persist in telling.

- Young children may not possess the language to express their upset or confusion. They may lack the actual words and so what they say does not carry the meaning they want to communicate. Adults may also not understand what a child is trying to tell them, or the possible meaning may seem so unlikely that the adult does not take real notice.
- Adults or young people who abuse sometimes make direct physical threats that ensure children's silence. The abuser may threaten to hurt the child if they tell, or make realistic threats towards someone else for whom the child cares.
- Abusers also make emotional threats, which can be just as effective as physical ones. They may say that, if the child tells, then the family will break up or the abuser will lose his job. Sexual abusers may claim that nobody will believe the child or that others will think the child is 'bad' or 'dirty'. The aim of these emotional threats is usually to make the child feel inappropriately responsible for any unhappy consequences of telling – 'It will be all your fault!'
- Children who have long experiences of abuse may simply assume that this is normal. They believe that it happens in all families or that it happens to 'bad' children like themselves who deserve ill-treatment.
- Children who are having difficulty telling, for whatever reason, may try to tell in ways that are hard for adults to 'hear'. Perhaps the child says very little or makes a throwaway comment that could be taken several different ways. S/he will not say any more if the adult's reaction is uninterested or dismissive.

When parents or other adults say something

Worries that may have child protection implications can arise because of what an adult tells you. A parent may speak to you about her/his own child or concerns s/he has about another child. The parent may be expressing direct worries that something is amiss. Alternatively, what s/he says could ring warning bells for you because it links in with other incidents or information, unknown to this parent.

The concerns may relate to this parent as an individual, to his/her partner or another family member or to other people involved with the family; to what another child in your centre is doing or to what this parent wishes to tell about the other child's family; or to the actions of a worker or volunteer in the setting.

Sometimes it will be an adult other than a parent who confides in you. Concerns might be raised by one of your colleagues, a volunteer or another professional who regularly visits your setting, such as a doctor, speech therapist or child psychologist.

A positive approach when an adult tells you something of concern has many features in common with good communication with children.

- Listen with care to what you are being told. Give this adult your full attention and ensure that you understand what is being said to you.
- Ask open-ended questions in the same way as described on page 88 for listening to children. You might repeat part of what the adult has said, but with a question in your tone or a few words of encouragement. For example, you might answer with 'So, you've seen Marsha's Mum hit the child a lot recently?' or 'You say you're really worried about the baby. Tell me what's worrying you so much.'
- You do not have to work out the truth of what you are hearing at this point. You should take seriously what you are told even if what the parent says seems unlikely to you or you do not want to believe it.
- Listen carefully and do not dismiss what you are told, even if the general view is that this parent is a gossip, dislikes the accused person or tends to make a fuss. A parent, or a member of staff, who raises many child protection worries that prove to be unfounded needs to be challenged in private conversation by a senior member of staff. There may be a number of possible underlying explanations, for instance, this

adult may believe an unrealistically high estimate about the prevalence of child abuse or s/he may be seeking attention through raising concerns. Frustrations with such a person should not be handled by automatically disbelieving them.

- An adult may ask you to keep what they say a secret or ask that you promise to keep their name out of any further enquiries. You cannot make either of these promises. Remind them of your setting's policy and obligation to pass on any concerns about children. You may also be able to reassure them that your next step will be to talk with your senior; you will *not* phone the police or social services without further consideration.

The Limits to Confidentiality

Adults who are the first to raise child protection concerns are often understandably worried about the personal consequences this will entail. You and your colleagues may feel just as uneasy as a parent who approaches you with such a worry.

However, social services cannot go ahead with a case if the only concerns being expressed are by anonymous sources. The process is very different from investigative journalism, when a newspaper article may well present some evidence without naming the source. Furthermore, local authority guidelines stress the importance of an open and accountable process; concerns cannot be entered or used as supporting material in an investigation if the informants are anonymous. It is also likely that parents will know, or have a good idea, who has expressed worries about them or their children. No possible useful work is going to be done with a family in your setting unless you own any concerns you voice.

The NSPCC are willing to accept anonymous referrals, although they prefer to have as much detail as possible. If you are talking to a parent who insists on keeping his/her name out of a report, you could advise them to contact the local NSPCC, but it would be sensible for you to inform your senior worker of the conversation.

Consulting colleagues

Concerns that are relevant to children's well-being should be shared appropriately in your setting. Your first step may vary, depending on the nature of your concern, exactly what you have noticed or what someone else has expressed to you. Some possibilities are:

- You may discuss what you have heard or noticed with your room colleague, so that you can both gain some perspective and draw on your more general knowledge of the child and family. Such a conversation must, of course, be confidential and out of the hearing of children and parents. This kind of discussion is not appropriate for general staff room conversation, snatched exchanges in corridors or the toilets.
- Pressing concerns should be discussed the same day with a senior worker or your head of centre. If you are yourself a senior worker, you might still want to talk in confidence with someone. A head of centre might welcome a conversation with the deputy, in order to weigh up what has been brought to her/his attention.
- Sometimes it is wise to raise a worrying pattern of concerns in a room meeting or some other centre group in which you discuss the progress and behaviour of individual children. However, you should not postpone serious concerns until you have a scheduled meeting.
- Persistent but vague worries about a child, parent or a colleague might be best raised during supervision, when a senior worker should help you to explore exactly what is troubling you and what might be done.
- Large early years centres may have a designated officer who specialises in child protection. Schools should have such a person because it was required by Circular 10/95 (see page 50), but in many early years or playwork settings you would talk with the head of centre.

Most of the possibilities outlined above highlight how important it is that general good practice is in place in your setting before there is a crisis, or potential crisis, in child protection. All early years settings need a positive atmosphere in which workers feel able to talk about concerns for the children, even if those worries are vague and hard to identify. Workers should support one another and senior workers specifically support the staff through informal conversations as well as regular supervision.

Support and supervision

You may be the colleague or senior worker to whom another worker turns for advice. You can support them by using effective communication:

- Listen to what the other person is telling you, without prejudging the issue one way or another. (You will notice that the advice to listen continues to come up throughout this section.) Child protection is a sensitive and emotional topic and listening with care is a good way to avoid premature conclusions: rejecting or accepting the reality of a worry on a mainly emotional basis.

- Ask questions that encourage the worker to say anything else that is relevant but do not direct too much. You might ask 'What else did he say to you?', 'Did she give you any more details about the baby's screaming?' or 'What sense do you make of this – given what you know of the child?'
- A worker who comes with a vague, although persistent concern, may need some help in exploring the worry. You might comment 'I understand you feel that Joan [a colleague] humiliates the children. Can you give me an example of what you mean – something that's happened recently?' or 'You say that this morning brought your worries about Karen to a head. Can you talk me through what happened – step by step?'
- You are not trying to make a final assessment of the truth of any concerns. As a more senior worker you are gaining an impression of what has happened and what has been said, given your general knowledge of this child, family or worker.
- Encourage the other worker to make their notes on the conversation now, if this work has not yet been completed.
- Support this worker in preparing how s/he will speak to the parent(s). The issue needs to be raised with the parent(s), if it was not them who approached the worker in the first place. If matters have arisen because of something the parent said, then the worker needs to be ready to speak to them about what will, or will not, be happening as a result in the centre.

If you work on your own

Your options may be far more limited if you work in a very small setting or are working on your own as a nanny or childminder. You may not have a senior with whom you can talk but every local area must have an Under-Eights Advisor (or someone with a similar title). As a childminder, you should be registered with the local social services under the Children Act 1989 or you may have the name of someone with specific responsibility for the childminding service.

Nannies are not required to be registered unless they are working with three or more families. However, nannies can still phone the local Under-Eights Advisor. Many of the national children's charities, including the NSPCC, have helplines that can support you in making sense of your concerns if there is nobody with whom you can talk in confidence.

Continued working relationships with parents or co-workers can be delicate or difficult in an early years setting where workers should find support from colleagues, but may be especially hard when you are working alone as a childminder in your own home or as a nanny in a family's home. Depending on what has happened, you may find that the working relationship, or your job if you are a nanny, is no longer viable. However, if you are relating to the non-abusing parent in a family abuse case, or if the abuser is from outside the family, your continuing relationship with the parent(s) may be a very welcome support to them.

Talking with parents

Assuming that it has not been the parent(s) who have spoken to you regarding a concern, it is good practice to discuss the matter with them as soon as possible after the problem or concern has arisen. The only valid reason for not talking to the parents before taking any other steps would be that you and your senior genuinely believe that the child is at risk from the parent. In such a case, your judgement, on the basis of sound information that you can explain clearly to other professionals, is that the child's immediate safety requires that you contact social services to set other procedures in motion.

If there is any doubt in your setting about talking with parents as the most usual first step, then remember that communication with parents, or children's other primary carers, represents good practice, in line with the Children Act 1989. This Act is the most important piece of legislation guiding child protection and key principles of the Act support parental responsibility and working in an active partnership with parents (see Chapter 2).

Whatever the nature of your concern, the conversation with a parent is unlikely to be easy or comfortable. However, you may get a straightforward and credible explanation to a difficult question, for instance about a child's injury. The parent may be pleased that you have spoken up because s/he shares your concerns and wants to do something about them. The appropriate action may not need to go further than your setting because no child protection concern arises – the key issues may concern the child's development or an understandable behavioural reaction to family stress or bereavement.

The value of partnership with parents

Without doubt it will be easier for you to have this kind of conversation if you have taken the trouble to establish a friendly working relationship with parents. Such a relationship gives parents a different context in which to make sense of your question about Sandra's bruises on her thigh or Mike's puzzling remark about 'seeing a strange man's willy'.

Perhaps you have taken time over the previous weeks or months to ask the parent's opinion on matters relating the child. You may have asked about non-confrontational personal matters such as food preferences or ways that you and the parent together might boost the child's physical confidence. Conversations of this kind will have established you as someone who relates to the child as an individual and to parents as people who matter.

There may have been incidents in the setting when you have had to explain to a parent how the child sustained a minor injury and what was done at the time. Alternatively the incident might have been one in which the child became emotionally upset about a story or an altercation between other children. This openness creates a two-way relationship where you have shown you believe that parents have a right to explanations.

Your previous approach will make it more likely that a parent will react positively to your query. A good working relationship with parents may also mean that Mike's mother tells you, without your having to ask, that yesterday she and her son had an unpleasant encounter with a flasher in the park or Sandra's father describes how his daughter fell out of the tree-house at the weekend.

You should never avoid talking with parents because:

- You are too busy. You must make the time and, if necessary, rearrange your time in order to have uninterrupted conversations with parents.
- You are concerned, perhaps for good reason, that the parent will get angry or abusive. Being shouted at is not a pleasant experience but you need to face this possibility for the sake of the child. See page 100 about an assertive approach.
- You cannot believe that anything like this could possibly happen in this family, so you are going to ignore the whole incident. There are no certainties as regards abusers in child protection work.
- You are worried about the consequences if your concerns are groundless, that you will spoil a friendly relationship with the parent

that has been hard to establish. One of the criticisms of poor social work practice has been that workers placed a good relationship with the parent as a higher priority than the welfare of the child. The Children Act stresses that the welfare of the child must be the most important consideration and should therefore take priority over adult feelings.

- You want somebody else to deal with the difficulty and so you refer the concern immediately to the social worker on the grounds that s/he will sort out the matter if there is anything serious. This step is not appropriate and would be bad practice. A simple conversation with a parent might clear up the questions, whereas going straight to social services without good reason will immediately place matters on a more serious footing, and undermine trust between the setting and the parents.

Assertive communication

Anything that you say to parents needs to be in your own words and to come across as a genuine communication. There is no format that is always right or that will avoid any awkwardness or unpleasantness, but there are better, as well as unwise, ways of expressing your concern or question. Your aim is for clear, honest and **assertive** communication. You need to avoid both a passive, unduly apologetic approach or an aggressive and confrontational line.

Be Clear in Your Own Mind

Decide what you want to tell or ask a parent (or other relevant carer).

- What exactly is puzzling you about what the child said or did?
- Where are the bruises, cuts or other marks and how did they come about?
- What patterns of behaviour from the child have concerned you? What is happening or not happening?

Which of your feelings are relevant and could appropriately be voiced? Some examples are:

- 'I'm uneasy about the games Jamie tries to play with two other children.'
- 'I'm confused about what Tara said. What kind of sense does it make to you as her mother?'
- 'I'm concerned that Alan is so often upset when your au pair picks him up. It's like he's a different child from the days when you or your husband come.'

It is unlikely to be appropriate to add apologies like 'I'm sorry but . . .' or riders like 'I'm sure there's a perfectly simple explanation' or 'Please don't think I'm interfering but . . .' The communication will be more straightforward if you express the facts and any relevant feelings simply. The time when it is appropriate to apologise is if there has been an accident at the centre involving the child or something has happened that should not have occurred. For instance, if one parent's child was inadvertently left in a locked classroom when the rest of the nursery group were taken off to see a video.

Practise if it Helps

If you feel it would help, then take the time to discuss with a colleague or senior worker what you will say to a particular parent at the end of the session or day. A second perspective can be helpful if you feel uneasy about the impending conversation or if you are not coming to terms with your difficulties in working out what you will say.

You could practise what you will say, either in your head or out loud with a colleague. Keep your message simple, for instance, 'Wai has several big bruises on her upper arms. Do you know how they came about?' Or 'Davie said an odd thing to me today. He said, "The ghosties will get me if I tell about Uncle Ned". He seemed very upset. What sense do you make of it?'

When the parent arrives to pick up the child:

- Ask to have a word in private if it is not easy to talk away from other parents and children.
- If the parent wants to rush off, you may need to press with, 'I appreciate you're in a hurry, but I think this is too important to wait until tomorrow/next week.'
- Say what you have to say and listen to the parent's reply.
- Be ready to repeat your question or statement if the parent does not seem to have listened or understood.
- Have a conversation that opens up the topic and be ready to make an arrangement to talk further with the parent in the very near future, if this seems appropriate.

Accidental or non-accidental injury?

There are no certainties in any guidelines over non-accidental injury but there are a number of features in a conversation with a parent that could put your mind at ease, or alternatively add to your existing concern. The same considerations hold if you are a senior worker in conversation with a member of staff who was responsible for the group when an accident happened.

Children can inflict a range of injuries on themselves without adult intervention. Every early years setting will have had accidents, sometimes serious, in a setting that is supposedly child-centred and child-friendly. So, it is important to remain open-minded and not to leap to conclusions because you do not like or trust the parent or worker. But also do not convince yourself it must be alright in order to avoid a difficult conversation.

Injury of a child as the result of a genuine accident is likely to have some or most of the following features:

- The parent (or other carer) acted swiftly to help the child, with appropriate first aid or seeking further medical help. Some people are prone to panic, but what happened after the panic subsided?
- After a full conversation, the explanation of the child's injury makes sense given the nature of the injury, the child's age, what you know of the child (some children are reckless) and their overall development. But again do not just be persuaded by your knowledge that this child seems without fear – was he being properly supervised?
- The description of the incident given by all the individuals involved, including the child if s/he is old enough to talk about what happened, is very similar, i.e. there is a consistent story.
- The child's appearance and demeanour do not suggest that s/he is fearful of his parent or neglected by them.

You would suspect non-accidental injury if the pattern varied significantly from the above, but be aware that genuine anxiety of parents can show itself in many ways. People are generally very aware of child abuse and so parents, in a family where no abuse has occurred, may seem uneasy. Perhaps they are genuinely worried that matters may get out of hand and that they will be accused of maltreatment.

The results of talking with parents

You may talk with parents and receive a reasonable and plausible explanation of what had concerned you. Good practice would still be to make a note in the child's record of the conversation. This is easier if you and the parents have a continuing relationship of openness and shared written records.

Alternatively your concern may not be put to rest. Perhaps what the parent says only adds to your concern, or the parent is relieved you have opened the subject and makes a disclosure about themselves or someone else involved with the family. The same guidelines for good communication apply as were outlined on page 88, including the reminder that you cannot keep a disclosure about possible abuse as a secret. Tell parents what you will be doing next and when you will speak with them again.

If you are a group worker, your next responsibility may be to speak with your senior. A senior worker or head of centre may need to consult with other workers whose input is relevant. Or, the decision might be that the head needs to consult the local Under-Eights Advisor or duty social worker. Within an early years setting, sharing of information should be on a 'need to know' basis. Concerns should not be voiced in general conversation in the staff room but workers who share the responsibility for a group of children all need to be fully informed of the situation.

Observations, records and reports

The material in this, and the following section, 'Working with other professionals', does overlap with others in this book. It is necessary, however, to place these important issues within the context of exactly how they are dealt with in early years settings.

Good practice

Observation and record keeping is an integral part of quality standards for early years work and your contribution to child protection will draw on this area of work.

As an early years worker, you should be observant of the children – what they do, what they enjoy and how individual children usually react. You will not notice everything in a busy group, but you should be alert to what is happening and be ready to focus your attention on individual children or activities.

Informal, daily observations of children through your contact in the setting should be complemented by more structured observations that build up a descriptive record of children's development and behaviour. Any setting should be able to make a substantial contribution to questions about a child's physical well-being, development and patterns of behaviour. You are *not* tracking children in your setting just in case child protection becomes an issue. What is needed is a positive focus on what children are able to do and how their development progresses over time. This focus will be the most helpful to any children who are at risk.

Child protection inquiries following the serious injury or death of a child have sometimes emphasised the danger, and perhaps tragic outcome, of nobody appearing to have kept track of the children themselves. Perhaps the professionals involved have been weighing up the parents' abilities to cope, the likely truth of competing explanations of what has happened or subtle issues of cultural patterns. In all these important facets of child protection monitoring, somebody must focus on the child. When children are attending an early years setting, your records and observations may contribute that crucial focus.

If you become concerned about a child, then do not wait for other professionals to ask for your contribution. Be ready to offer the perspective that your setting can bring to the child's well-being and perhaps their safety. If you are a senior worker or head of centre, then make sure that you develop contacts within the local child protection system (see page 70). As a senior, it is also your responsibility to develop your team so that workers feel confident to present their observations and summarise their records of a child.

The contribution of an early years setting will not be the final word on whether a child is being abused. Your input will be part of informal early inquiries or a more detailed investigation. Early years workers should be able to contribute to a discussion, with the support of a child's records. Your contribution may support the concern about a child or may place isolated concerns in a more positive context. Two examples follow.

Example One

'Yes, we have become concerned about Emma's behaviour. When we look back through our records for her, she seems to have become more and more unhappy over the last two months. She is tearful and gets upset about minor difficulties when nobody is cross with her at all. During the last fortnight, her key worker has noticed that Emma has been picking at her skin so much that she has raw patches around her finger nails and on her scalp. This week we approached Emma's mother with our concerns, but we haven't got much further than her Mum saying that there are what she calls "family troubles" at the moment.'

Example Two

'No, we're not worried about Hamid's weight. Our records for the last six months show that he has made steady gains and he eats a balanced diet. His general health is good and minor scratches heal quickly. When we observe his play, Hamid has plenty of energy and he keeps up with children of his own age. The health visitor is right to say that Hamid is on the lowest percentile for the standard weight charts, but the entire family is shorter and smaller than average. Hamid had some frustrations when a couple of children tried to baby him in their games but he's been able to deal with that, with some discreet help from his key worker. We are happy to keep monitoring Hamid, but we want to avoid the weight business becoming a big issue. Hamid's mother asked to speak with the key worker this week and she seems to feel harassed by all the visits and questions about her son.'

Records and child protection

When child protection becomes an issue, good standards in written reports apply in the same way as with any other issue. You should consider:

- *What* you need to record.
- The reasons *why* you are recording this information.
- Good practice in *how* you record.
- Issues of *confidentiality* of reports and of *appropriate access* to them.

Factual Information

Good written records must be factual. Opinions are important, as long as they are supported (see later in this section), but a good and useful report does not confuse facts with opinions and interpretations.

Your written record has to report the facts as they are known. This emphasis is crucial whether you are writing a few sentences of notes in an on-going record or several pages in a summary report on a child. You should consider the following:

- What happened, where and when? Give dates and times if appropriate.

For example: perhaps a teenage brother has been observed to hit and drag the younger sibling he collects from nursery. Who saw this incident? When did it occur? What happened before the blow was struck? Where were the siblings when the elder struck the younger one? Has there been more than one similar incident? What, if anything, did anyone from the nursery do or say?

- If a child's behaviour has concerned you, then describe what you observed. Support your observation with an explanation, not necessarily very long, of your reasons for concern. If your concern focuses on a pattern of behaviour or observable changes in a child's more usual reactions, then exactly what have you seen or heard, and when?
- If you write up what someone else has told you, perhaps a parent or concerned neighbour, then make it clear in your report when you are documenting what somebody else says they have observed.

For example: you may not have direct experience that 'Emma's parents are having awful rows'. More accurately, what you are reporting is that 'Emma's next-door neighbour [name] spoke with me on [date] to say that he is "very worried" because he hears "all these screaming matches" through the wall between his home and the Davisons.'

You may have direct observations of your own which would tend to support the view that there are serious disruptions going on in Emma's family. Perhaps you went to the home corner because the children's play was getting very noisy and were told by Emma, 'But Damian's being the Daddy. He has to shout.'

- Only quote somebody else's words if you are sure that this is exactly what was said, whether s/he is a child or adult. If you are uncertain of the exact words then be honest and write that the child, or adult said 'something like . . .' Do not tidy up a child's words, or those of an adult. If what was said is open to more than one interpretation, then this ambiguity must be maintained. The more prompt you are in writing up your notes, the more accurate your memory will be.
- If a child's physical well-being is in question then be specific about your observations. Perhaps a child regularly arrives in winter time wearing lightweight summer clothes. Note down the days and what the child is wearing, do not leave a vague note such as 'Gabrielle's clothes are inadequate for the weather.'
- If a child has injuries, then make an accurate record of the nature and extent of the bruises, cuts or other marks. You could use a simple outline figure of a child, front and back versions, to sketch the location

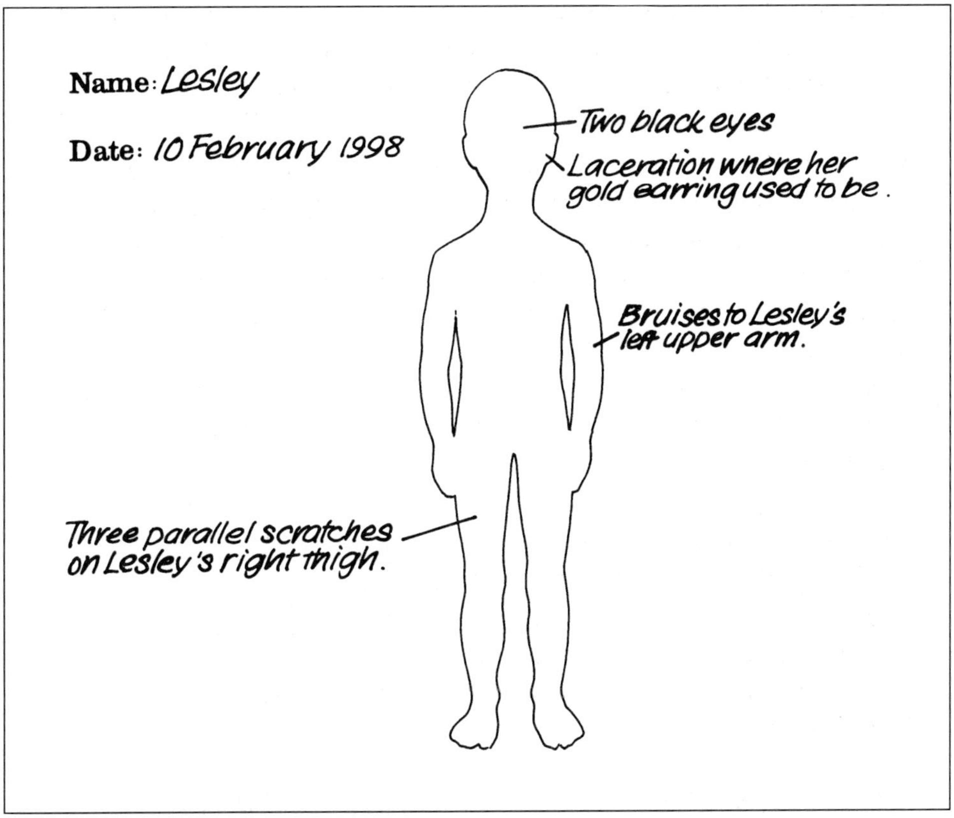

Using a body outline in records
See Appendix 1, page 171 for a photocopiable outline

of any injuries. Do not draw any conclusions that you are unable to support, and do not make guesses about the possible cause of any injury.

> *For example*: you might write that 'there were four bruises on Ansel's upper arm and one under the arm'. You should not claim that the marks are from a fierce grip on the child's arm unless you have a sound reason. A series of small, round, inflamed marks on Ansel's back might be cigarette burns, but what independent evidence do you have? If you have no basis for a considered guess, then do not go any further than a description in your report.

- Use only sketches and a written description, unless the child protection team specifically asks you to take photographs (and this is very unlikely). Assessment in a child protection inquiry does sometimes involve photographic evidence, and anyone involved in such an inquiry must be aware of children's dignity and their right not to be subjected to more intrusive investigation or recording than is absolutely necessary.

- Write down as literally as you can any explanation that the child gives about the injury, and in the same way, what the parent says when you approach him/her.

> *For example*: your observation of a lacerated area on a child's leg, and discussions with those involved, might then be supported with the notes that, 'Sian and her father both said that the family dog bit Sian on Saturday night. Mr Evans told May [key worker] that he took Sian to Casualty immediately. The doctor cleaned the wound but said that no stitches were necessary.'
>
> Another explanation by a different parent might leave you with doubts that need to be expressed in the report. For example, 'Max's mother says that she left the hot iron on the floor for a moment and that Max backed into it. I am still concerned about the way in which Max received this burn, because the shape on his lower back is the opposite way round to an iron when it is resting' (with a diagram of the shape of the child's burn on his body).

Timely Recording

You should make your notes as soon as possible after your observation and certainly within the same day. The longer you leave it to make your written record, the greater the chance that you will forget details. You may also start to lay your own interpretation over events.

Timely recording is an important issue for all professionals; it does not only affect early years workers. For instance, if child protection, or any other cases, reach court, then professionals giving evidence are often asked to be specific about exactly when they made their notes. Records written up many days after important events are far less credible than those that are promptly recorded.

Support your Opinions

You, and your colleagues, have personal experience of individual children and a broad base of knowledge about child development in general. You will draw on one or both of these sources when you weigh up, with colleagues or your senior, to what extent there is cause for concern. The important point is that you share, through your written record, how you reached a judgement and do not simply give the judgement itself, such as, 'we should be worried' or 'there's no cause for concern'.

Factual description is vital in reports relevant to child protection but your opinions are also of value, as long as you give reasons for your opinions. Some of the examples already given in this section include supported opinions. There is a great deal of difference, in terms of the credibility of the report, between 'Fazila's parents neglect her' and 'We have been concerned about the standard of Fazila's care from her family because she wears the same clothes, including underwear, for over two weeks at a time. Fazila has become distressed because other children do not want to sit next to her and say that she smells. Fazila is in regular pain with her teeth, which we have mentioned on three occasions [dates] to her mother but there is no sign that the child has been taken to the dentist. Fazila is usually very hungry on Monday mornings and eats several helpings at breakfast. Her hunger seems to lessen as the week goes by . . .' And so on.

Sometimes it is not easy to ascertain exactly what it is that concerns you. It is important to pursue any strong feelings of unease and a colleague or your senior, within a supervision session, may be able to help you. It might also help to be asked questions such as, 'Can you describe for me the most recent time that you felt very uneasy about this child?' Open-ended questions will help you be more specific about who was present, what happened or who said what.

Your uneasiness may be fuelled by what does not happen. For instance, perhaps a child's mother rarely seems to react in one way or another – happiness when the child is excited or sympathy if the child is distressed. You could not conclude from this that the child was necessarily subject to deliberate emotional abuse: the mother might be severely depressed or under a great deal of stress.

It is often possible, with the help of a colleague, to identify the firmer observational basis of a gut feeling. This observation can then be written into the report. If you cannot identify firmer ground then you should not write vague and unsupported feelings in a report, such as 'Nobody in Liam's family seems to care about him' or 'I'm certain there is something very wrong in the Brownlow family.' If you cannot support a comment, then do not write it in the report. You are leaving yourself, and the centre whom you represent, open to accusations of unfairness to a family or prejudice against the parents on some grounds. And, if you are expressing criticisms with no obvious evidence, then perhaps you are working from unreasonable or ill-informed assumptions about this family.

Clear Written Style

Records need to be written in a clear and concise style – child protection reports are no different in that way from any written record in your setting:

- If your records are handwritten, make sure that your writing is legible and check the spelling of words if you have any doubt; if you work on a word processor, then make sure that you use the spell-check function.
- Make it easy for anyone to follow the flow of your report: ensure that any narrative about a child or family goes in the right order, with dates or times next to the incidents in question.
- Use headings if that is appropriate, and consider making a list of bullet points for clarity if you are describing a series of incidents or concerns. It can be easier to follow this kind of list than a description within one long paragraph.

If you are a senior worker, be ready to support your team in the improvement of their style in written reports. Offer them specific suggestions on how they could improve a particular report and avoid non-specific criticisms. For instance, it is very discouraging for a worker to be told bluntly 'Your report is far too muddled. You'll have to re-organise it before we let the social worker see it.' You could be more helpful in your feedback with 'I find the report hard to follow because your different concerns about Tom appear in bits throughout the report; and your descriptions are often separate from the dates you give. You seem to have three main concerns, so let's see if you can gather together your information on each one. Let's start with your worry about Tom and the games he tries to play with Natalie.'

Confidentiality and Access

Parents should know the centre's policy on records, because you should have given them this information early on in the relationship, and a clear statement about records should be part of written material on the centre. Parents should have straightforward access to the records of their own children. Anyone else should only have access on a clear 'need to know' basis. If child protection issues are raised then the children's records, or more usefully, summaries of them could well become an important part of material on the child and family. The setting's developmental records of children might be a crucial support in assessments of whether a child's development and behaviour is a source of concern or not.

When you write records it is important to remind yourself that parents will be able to read what you are writing. Do not be less honest because of this realisation but be ready to support everything you write.

Talking about reports

Other professionals may read your full reports on a child and a clear, well written report will make their task easier. Good quality reports will also support a confident stance with your local child protection team that early years settings have a vital contribution to make to the process. You may find that your own local team is only too ready to involve your setting and listen to your perspective. However, some readers of this book will undoubtedly have to establish themselves with other professionals who are less than positive about the input of early years settings. Make sure that your contribution to the process is professional.

At some point, you might have to present a summary of your report on a child to a group of other professionals, perhaps at a case conference. It may not be appropriate to work your way through the entire record. Prepare yourself before the meeting and make summary notes that will guide you. You will probably need to cover the following:

- The nature of your concern about the child.
- Information supporting your concern.
- What you have done in your setting with the child and parents.
- Any changes, for better or not, that you have observed in the child.

It may also be worth communicating clearly to the meeting that the centre would welcome suggestions for further work with the child or parents, and that you would like, and expect, to be kept informed so that you can contribute to the protection of this child.

Working with other professionals

The Children Act 1989 makes it a legal requirement that different agencies work together for the well-being of children. Reviews of good, and poor, practice in child protection have stressed the importance of people from different professional backgrounds and agencies working in co-operation and mutual respect.

If the concern about a child arises within your setting, then the head of centre will make the decision about contacting someone outside the setting. Sharing your concerns with other professionals should be done with the parents' knowledge, since you should have spoken with the parent(s) as soon as you became concerned. The parent(s) may not always be happy about you passing on your concerns – they might prefer that you kept silent – but they should be informed about the steps you are taking.

There are few circumstances in which you would be justified in immediately contacting another professional without a discussion with the child's parent(s). You might call the police if a parent were attacking the child or members of staff in your setting; or you might call a doctor if a child was seriously injured or showed signs of needing urgent medical attention. Talk with members of your local child protection team for some clear guidance on any circumstances that they feel would justify an immediate call to the team. From the perspective of early years settings, the features of good inter-professional co-operation are:

- Knowing your role and that of other professionals in the bigger picture of child protection. Working to understand the boundaries of your role: what you do and when you should hand over to another professional.
- Setting up regular channels of communication so that you have established some professional links before a crisis (see also page 69).
- Working to be assertive and confident in your professional approach and, if you are a senior worker, supporting your team in becoming more confident about your contribution to child protection.
- Knowing what the child protection team's expectations of your centre are as regards your work with this individual child and family. What, exactly, would they like you to do and with what goals in mind? When should you be reporting back?
- Knowing exactly what other members of the team will be doing. Who is taking the lead responsibility on this case?

You may all need to address doubts about how early years work is regarded by other professionals in your local area. You cannot force other professionals to change their minds if they undervalue the contribution of early years settings but you can, by consistently behaving in a professional manner, make it harder for them to hold this view.

- Be proactive and offer your opinion through carefully considered words and good written reports.

- If you are finding the child protection team resistant to recognising the importance of early years settings, talk to your local Under-Eights Advisor. See if you can mobilise some extra support for your efforts.
- Speak up in meetings rather than complaining afterwards that you were not asked for your opinion. Make sure that you, or the setting's representative, is prepared to speak about a child or family. Show your knowledge and considered opinion about the child.
- Act in advance by ensuring that the representative of your setting has a slot on the agenda of the meeting. Talk with the chair of the meeting or find out from your Under-Eights Advisor whom you should contact.
- Make sure that all these moves are undertaken in the professional spirit of co-operation. Avoid resentment at not being contacted or considered. If your contribution has been overlooked, it may not have been a deliberate slight by the child protection team. Early years settings still have to establish themselves against a strong tradition of undervaluing care.
- Within meetings or discussions at your setting, make it clear that you will keep communications open with other professionals and that you are confidently expecting the same courtesy. You would not expect to be contacted on a daily basis about a child, but you should be given updates so that you know what is happening with the child and family and you can review your work in the setting.
- In any work that is part of the child protection process, you will need to establish common goals and discuss any apparent differences in approach or terminology. But respect any remaining differences between your work and that of the other professionals, including social workers. Your roles are not the same.

Case studies

These are short examples of the kinds of situations you might face. For each example, consider one or more of the following questions. (Do not feel you have to work through them all in one sitting.)

1 What might you say to the child in this situation? Practise actual phrases rather than general ideas. You could make notes or try out a sentence with a colleague or fellow-student.
2 What will you say to the parent at the end of the day or session? Again, try some actual sentences. In a group, you could work some examples into a short role play, with the support of your tutor.

3 What should you say to a more senior worker? Or what should you raise, if you are the more senior worker and your team do not seem to take the situation seriously?
4 Should you make a note of what has happened? If so, what key points should you note?

Sergio

Four-year-old Sergio has been persistently trying to grope the female workers in your centre. When you started at the centre two weeks ago, you were warned never to turn your back on the boy, but this was explained as 'macho Italian stuff – it's the family'. Within a week you have noticed how workers stand with their back to the fence out in the garden and a couple have held Sergio away. Today, Sergio tried to push his hand up your T-shirt.

Sally

A parent asks to speak with you. Sally, her child, is not in your group, but in one run by Ian and Jessica. She says, 'I know it's awkward to ask you, but I'm worried that Ian is leaving. We've always been a bit concerned about Jessica. She's very fierce with the children. Sally says some amazing things when she's playing with dolls, and it's not the kind of stuff that we say to her. Ian seemed to keep the balance, but now he's going. Could you get our daughter moved into your group?'

Rory

Rory is two years old and seems to have a lot of accidents at home. His mother, who runs her business from home, has offered a reasonable explanation for each incident so far. You know Rory as a bold child whose curiosity and self-confidence can lead him into risky situations even in the day nursery. This morning Rory has a very large bruise on his forehead and you ask his mother what happened. She replies, 'I think he pulled out the kitchen steps to get to the biscuits. He must have fallen off. It was a while before I realised.' You ask, 'Oh, weren't you in the kitchen with him then?' She looks a bit embarrassed and then says firmly, 'I had an assignment to finish. I can't turn down work, you won't have them after 6.30 and his father won't watch him.'

Owen

In a conversation over lunch at your centre, three-year-old Owen is talking about the new baby that will come soon. Owen is talking with affection, 'I pat the baby in Mummy's tummy. Her tummy's very big and knobbly. I see it in the bath.' Your colleague asks Owen with some surprise, 'Do you and Mummy have a bath together?' He replies, 'Oh, yes. We have wet cuddles in the bath.' You have never been concerned about Owen or his family but your colleague talks with you later over coffee. She says, 'Don't you think we should report this. People shouldn't have baths with their children. It isn't right.' She shudders and looks very uncomfortable.

Yvette

Yvette is seven years old and attends your after-school club. Her mother dresses Yvette is what you feel are inappropriate clothes for a girl of her age. She wears mainly crop tops, tight short skirts and her shoes often have little heels. Yvette wears nail polish and has three earrings in each ear. You have become increasingly uneasy hearing Yvette's comments about someone called Martin. Yvette has said things like 'I'm his little princess' and 'Martin is going to get me a CD player if I'm good.' Yvette seems to have become even more flirty with your male colleague than previously. He has just said to you that Yvette wanted to sit on his lap this afternoon. He made an excuse to get her off, because she seemed to be wriggling back very firmly against his crotch.

Winston

Fifteen-month-old Winston often seems to be grumpy in the morning but today he is very out of sorts and wanders around in a daze until lunch time. When his mother picks him up you ask whether Winston has been unwell. She replies, 'I think we overdid the sleeping medicine.' You look puzzled and she continues, 'Winston is an awful sleeper. My Mum said to give him a tot of sherry. She said that was what she used to do and it didn't do us any harm. I was having a terrible time and one night I started to shake him. So I thought the sherry would be safer.'

5

Working with Individual Children and Families

Children's experiences of abuse are very varied and so there is no single pattern of how best to help them. There are, however, some practical guidelines that enable early years workers to take a positive approach. Many of the suggestions in this section are grounded in good practice with all children, whether or not they have had distressing experiences.

Working with the children

Consult other professionals

Good contacts with the child protection team should include practical discussions about the contribution of the early years setting. If you are still building an effective working relationship, perhaps the centre will have to make some active moves. Do not just wait for the social worker to call you. You might want to ask about the following:

- Is there anything specific you would like us to do within the centre? Are there any particular checks on the child we should be carrying out, or is there anything within our records that might be helpful?
- What suggestions would you make about how best to help within the centre from your knowledge of the child and the family?
- It will be helpful to know whether other specialist input is being offered to the child or family. You are not asking for confidential details of counselling or therapy, but this information will support you in your relationship with the child and his/her family. With some shared information, you will perhaps learn the identity of 'Lisa' who apparently talks with this child every week or the 'clinic' that 'Mummy has gone to this weekend'.
- Early years workers should not attempt forms of therapy with children when they are inexperienced in such work, but there is much that you can do within your boundaries. The social worker might be able to advise you about what kinds of support would be most helpful.

Practical monitoring and physical care

Usual good practice in observation and physical care may be sufficient for some children who have experienced abuse. However, when a child has been injured or seriously neglected, the centre may be asked to monitor this child in a more specific way. You may be asked:

- To ensure that the child is brought into your setting for the agreed days or sessions, and to contact the appropriate person if the child is absent beyond a particular time.
- To check a child for bruises or new injuries. Make sure that any checking is done with respect for the child and an awareness of the sense of bodily dignity of even young children. Have an honest and simple answer ready for when a child asks you why you are undertaking these checks.
- To weigh children or keep a record of what they eat in your setting.
- To keep a record of the state of children's clothing and whether it is appropriate for the weather, or check that a young child is in a clean nappy or underwear.

Supporting the children

The key to effective support of children is to treat them as normally as possible, without pretending that nothing has happened.

You will not be able to treat children who have been abused in exactly the same way as children whose life experience has been less disruptive and distressing, but it would not be good practice, in any case, to attempt to treat all children in exactly the same way. Sensitive early years workers should respond to children as individuals, tuning in to what they say and being sensitive to how a child's abusive experience will be reflected in his/her play, conversation and behaviour. You should be able to draw on your general experience with children in order to assess how to work with and support a child who has been abused.

Affirm the Child as a Worthwhile Individual

An experience of abuse or neglect can make children seriously doubt themselves and the trustworthiness of adults. Children need to feel, or learn to feel, through positive experiences with adults, that someone cares about what happened and will support them from now on. You can help in the following ways:

- If children say critical things of themselves, you need to offer positive emotional support. Avoid simply saying 'It's not true' or 'You don't think that, really' as such responses are dismissive. Clearly the child does think such negative thoughts about him/herself, or has reason to believe that you might.
- You can acknowledge that the child has expressed a strong feeling with a phrase like 'It must be difficult for you to feel that way.' You do not have to agree with the child's negative remark but can say warmly, '*I* like you' or '*I* don't think you're a bad boy.'
- In your continuing relationship with the child, you can show your positive feelings not only through what you say, but also in how you behave towards the child. Smiles, encouraging nods and attention given to a child's comments and activities all communicate that you value him/her and like to have him/her in your group.
- You can express emotional warmth and affection to children who doubt themselves and also to children whose behaviour, shaped by their experience, is hard to handle in the group.
- As with all children, you should be guided by the child in how close they want an adult to be or how much they want to be touched. No adult should push a child further than the child wishes for hugs, hand holding, sitting on your lap or any other simple physical expression of closeness appropriate with young children.
- Take the time to draw in a very distrustful child and do not feel that your skills are in question. Some children may take a long time to open up and you have to be pleased with small successes.
- Children need your support and sympathy, but pity is rarely a helpful emotion to express to anyone in distress. Avoid talking about children in hushed tones or expressing pity through speech or body language.
- Make sure that you involve children in decisions and ask them for their opinion. Even if it takes time before a child believes you really mean what you say, keep trying.

Listen and be ready to talk

Children do not forget about distressing events just because adults avoid talking about them. What is more likely is that children will conclude, perhaps correctly, that the adults are reluctant to talk. In the absence of any clear message, children may also conclude that adults are cross with them or believe the children did something wrong or are dirty. Emotionally damaging thoughts can grow in a child's mind if nothing positive is being communicated by adults who should care.

Listen and be ready to talk in the following ways:

- It is important for you to provide children with a chance to express their feelings, but do not press them to talk at times or communicate in ways that are not the child's choice.
- Some children who have experienced abuse may want to talk to you. Others may never say much at all about their experiences. Their feelings and confusions may emerge through their play and you can help them in this way (see page 120).
- The guidelines on page 88 about listening, open-ended questions and being guided by the child will all be useful.
- Some children may tell you about events that not only distressed them, but also shake you when you hear the details. You may be stunned by a child's apparent indifference to a catalogue of ill-treatment, but she thinks this kind of misery is normal.
- Show your sympathy and acknowledge children's feelings. It can be appropriate to show a child that you are angry on their behalf or that what happened was not fair, but your own feelings must not overwhelm the time you spend with the child and your anger or distress on their behalf should not become a burden to them. If you have strong feelings that are hard to resolve, then find an opportunity to talk about your reactions and feelings with another adult within your centre.

Angie

Angie, who has seen angry rows between her parents, is talking to Jane, her key worker at the after-school club.

Angie: Do you shout at Mark [Jane's partner]?
Jane: No, I don't. We try to talk about things when we disagree.
Angie: Do you yell at Bella [Jane's child]?
Jane: No. I try hard not to.
Angie: My Mummy shouts at Daddy all the time.
Jane: Yes, I realise that. But not all Mummies and Daddies shout at each other.
Angie: Mummy yells at me and I haven't done anything.
Jane: Yes, I know. You hear a lot of shouting, don't you, Angie?
Angie: Mummy says I'm a 'useless little cow'.
Jane: I'm sorry your Mummy says that to you, Angie. I don't agree with her at all. You're a real help here and I like you very much.

And so on . . .

> **COMMENT:**
>
> Jane accepts Angie's questions about her own family life and answers honestly. Angie is asking and not prying. But if Angie were to ask inappropriately curious questions, Jane could decline to answer with a comment like, 'That's private to me.'

Support children through play

It is usual for children to weave personal experiences into their play, so events in the lives of children who are abused may also emerge through different play activities in your setting.

Unless you have specific skills in play therapy, you should not set out to use play with a child to help him/her through his/her experiences. However, a sensitive early years worker can be supportive by responding to opportunities that arise naturally. It is also important that you relate to abused children in play as you would to any child: enjoying their successes and satisfaction and looking for opportunities for them to learn. It is not helpful to seek deeper meanings in every drawing they do or find greater significance in rough physical play than you would for another child.

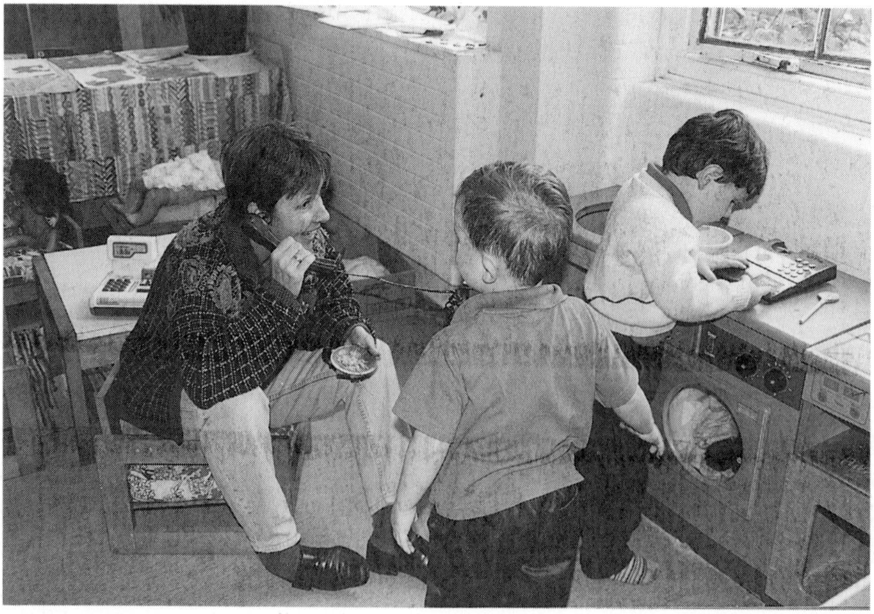

Supporting children through play

ACTIVITY

Consider what would be the most positive approach if you observed any of the following examples of a child's play. Questions to consider are:

- What might you say or do?
- How might you guide the child's play from this point onwards?
- Are there times when you might courteously stop the child in what s/he is saying or doing?
- When other children are involved, what might you say or do about their reaction?
- What might you note in the child's records, or pass on to your senior worker?

1 Kitty is four years old. There is a strong suspicion that she was sexually abused by her grandfather when he looked after her. The evidence was not certain, but Kitty's mother was worried enough to agree to ban the grandfather from their home. Kitty has said very little in the nursery but, when she is painting or drawing, sometimes she draws a figure on the paper then scribbles or paints all over it. Today she whispers to you, 'No more Grandad.'

2 The local child protection team is making initial inquiries about Marsha's family because of concerns that her mother is hitting her and the young baby in the family. Marsha is usually very quiet in the playgroup but today you hear her shouting in the home corner. When you go closer, you can see her violently shaking the baby doll and shouting, 'Be quiet! Be quiet!' Another child in the home corner is looking at Marsha with disapproval.

3 Joan, a worker in your children's centre, has been suspended following complaints of her bad practice. There are claims that Joan regularly humiliated and threatened children, and used unacceptable punishments, including shutting one child in a cupboard and making another child stand out in the rain. This afternoon you have watched a group of children play out what seem to be some of their experiences with this worker. The child who is playing Joan is shouting insults at the others and threatening, 'It'll be the wooden spoon for you!' The game comes to a close when the other children all leap on 'Joan' and shout, 'You're going to prison now.'

4 You are playing tea parties with Fazila who appears to enjoy making tea and laying out the table. Fazila lines up the dolls who are joining you both for tea, but she puts one doll at some distance from the others. You ask if this doll is coming to the tea party and Fazila replies, 'She's a smelly-

poo – nobody likes her.' You have been working with Fazila's mother to try to improve the child's care, but her clothes are still changed infrequently and there are some days when Fazila smells unwashed.

5 At break this morning, in the playground of the school where you work, you watched a vigorous physical game between the children that gradually began to concern you. The game involved a lot of shrieking and chasing in which the boys and girls were equally active. But one small group of boys, which appeared to be led by Sammy, seemed to push the game beyond the limits that some of the girls wanted. A couple of girls were pushed against the fence and kissed, although they were shouting, 'Stop it!' You cannot be sure, but it looked also as if Sammy was trying to put his hand up the skirt of one girl. Sammy is a child who has concerned you because of the sexually explicit jokes that he sometimes makes.

6 Every morning you have a circle time in which children can 'show and tell' any item of interest from their own lives. Today, Ansel got to his feet and told the group that his Mum had gone to a clinic, 'You know, because she drinks so much.' Ansel continued in a matter-of-fact tone, 'But Dad says it's a waste of time "cos she's such a boozer".' The other children look mildly surprised but interested.

Deal positively with behaviour

You need to act as a responsible adult with obligations to the whole group as well as to any children who have experienced abuse.

Children need your understanding of the impact of their distressing experiences and you may well have to adjust your expectations of the development, behaviour and outlook that you would usually attribute to a child of this age. But children will not benefit from a tolerance that is without limits and, in the long term, it will be unhelpful if they are permitted to behave in highly disruptive or unacceptable ways without any constructive reaction from adults. Workers may see the child's abusive experience as an excuse, or may be genuinely concerned that setting some limits to behaviour and having expectations of children may add to their burdens.

However, it can be very reassuring to a child to see that adults take responsibility and act in a predictable manner. Children whose lives have been very disrupted will probably need a predictable early years environment. They may have experienced unpredictable or highly punitive control from parents or other carers, and in some cases, unpredictability has been fuelled by the parents' use of alcohol or drugs. Such children may also need clear structure in their daily lives. It may be even more important to them than to the other children that they know exactly what will be happening and that there are no surprises.

You will need to be prepared for different reactions from children. Some children who have witnessed bouts of domestic violence may be distressed by even mild altercations or expect fierce words from you for minor mistakes. These children will need a great deal of reassurance as they learn that you do not react like their aggressive parent(s). They may need to hear this message directly from you, 'I'm not cross. Everyone makes mistakes sometimes' or 'It's not a big thing, Barry. We can put it right together.' Others may show the opposite behaviour: a readiness to use fierce words and aggressive actions. You will need to step in with a firm, 'It's alright to be cross. It's not alright to hit people.'

An abused child should not be allowed to get away with behaviour that would not be tolerated from another child. Nor should other children have to accept ill-treatment from a child because s/he has had bad experiences.

- Take a positive line in guiding this child's behaviour with the underlying message of 'I like you, Ansel. I don't like what you did to Marianne.'
- Offer alternatives for action and explain simply why one course of action is not allowed.
- Show and encourage other ways that a child might use to handle frustration, distress, showing affection or trying to make friends.
- Be practical on behalf of the child, always balancing 'please don't do that' with guidance in words and actions that say 'I'd rather you behaved this way' (see page 158).

Children who have been abused should not be allowed to mistreat other children because of their misery or anger. It is unfair to the other children and will not help the abused child in the long run. You should follow the same guidelines as you would with children who behave aggressively in the centre or whose family experience has taught them that they can have whatever they want, without regard for others.

When children have been sexually abused, they may bring inappropriate behaviour into the setting. The child may seek over-intimate contact with workers or with other children. You need to establish what can be a delicate balance between the messages of 'I like you and I am happy to have you close to me' and 'The way you want to touch me is not the right way between a child and an adult.'

Other children and parents in the group

When one child brings problems into a group, the other children may need to be reassured that you are aware of what is happening. They will feel that your behaviour is fair to everyone if they can see you deal with disruptive or inappropriate behaviour, and confident that you are taking responsibility for the group if you move swiftly to deal with a child's distress. Children can be protective and caring towards each other and may react well to simple explanations or behaviour that do not break confidences. For example, you might explain, 'It's okay Melissa, I know you didn't say anything mean to Cameron. But he gets upset if people shout at him. Just try saying things in a normal voice.'

If a child's abusive experience is emerging through misbehaviour in the group, you may also have to explain this to the parents of other children. Explanations should never become excuses and parents should not be expected to tolerate physical or emotional damage to their own children

Young children are often naturally affectionate towards each other

because another child is having problems. Explain simply to concerned parents that you are aware of what is happening, that you are taking steps to deal with the situation and that you appreciate their having spoken to you.

You should also be prepared to talk to children and their parents if there has been alleged or proven abuse by a worker, volunteer or visitor to the centre (see page 140).

Working with parents

Your work with parents may take several forms:

- Trying to continue a working relationship with a parent who is alleged to have abused or who has admitted ill-treating his/her child.
- Supporting a non-abusing parent who is distressed and confused because his/her partner has abused their child.
- Working with parents whose child has been abused by somebody else, either within the family, a trusted person allowed contact with the child or, less usually, a stranger.

Offering a welcome

A friendly face and a continued welcome to your setting may be exactly what some parents want and need. For parents whose life has been turned upside down, their child's nursery or preschool may be the one setting that remains constant. Non-abusing parents may really appreciate a place where they and their child are treated as normally as possible. You will be available to talk about the difficulties if they wish, but otherwise you are still there to show parents the collage their child completed or tell how s/he was such a help in reorganising the store cupboard.

Some parents may be angry because it was the centre that first raised concerns about possible abuse, but it is possible that you will get through the anger and be able to offer support (see 'Parents' feelings' later in this section). The anger of some parents does not, of course, subside and you will have to continue your contact with them in as civil a way as possible.

Others do not necessarily turn against their child's early years setting, even if it was you that first raised the concerns. They may feel that, despite mixed emotions about the centre, their key worker or the head of centre is basically on the side of their child and family and will be supportive.

A formal or informal parents' group may offer support to depressed or isolated parents whose stress and loneliness has contributed to the neglect of their children. Company or support from other parents and workers will not solve all their problems, but it can help.

Talking and listening

Some parents may wish to talk to you about what has happened and what they can expect. Use your skills of listening, of open-ended questioning and of offering ideas without telling parents what to do (see page 88). You can be helpful and still be honest about what you do not know and cannot make happen. You should not attempt detailed individual work, for instance trying to counsel parents, unless you genuinely have the time and have been trained in the appropriate skills.

A PRIVATE CONVERSATION

These supportive conversations should be private so you need to find a time to talk without the children in earshot. It is almost inevitable in a busy early years setting that you will have snatched conversations, but this is unwise. Parents may have deep and confused feelings, they may become distressed or angry (not necessarily with you) and they may talk about their child(ren) in the hearing of other children or parents. If what seemed to be a quick question about information is turning into what ought to be a longer private conversation, then you should halt the parent and say 'I want to give you some proper time, but it's impossible now. Can you can come back at . . .?'

PARENTS' FEELINGS

The strong feelings that parents express will vary between individuals and depend on the circumstances of the abuse, that is, the type of abuse, the alleged abuser and the emotional state of the child. There is no blueprint for how parents should feel. They may express any of the following emotions and these may change over time:

- Shock and an inability to take in what has happened. A non-abusing parent may still find it hard to believe what has occurred; an abusing parent may feel stunned that matters got so out of hand.
- Anger at someone who has abused their child. Or an abusing parent may feel angry that justifiable discipline has been called abuse or that a child's word is believed over an adult's counter-claim. Parents may feel angry with the person(s) who first raised the concerns, even if they also feel a sense of relief. Anger has to be directed somewhere and a non-abusing parent may initially find it hard to be angry with a

previously trusted partner or friend. Sometimes anger is directed, at least initially, towards the child. It is neither rational nor fair, but in a seriously disrupted household the child is sometimes blamed.

- Guilt at not realising earlier or not facing nagging worries about a child's physical or emotional state. A non-abusing parent may fret over why the child did not tell and you may need to explain the many reasons why children often do not speak up about physical or sexual abuse (see page 93). An abusing parent may feel very guilty about what has been done and may be willing to accept help, but not all abusers feel this way.
- Relief that the abuse has been discovered and is being challenged. A neglectful parent may feel many other emotions but still feel that it is better to get help than to struggle.
- Doubt in their own ability to protect their children. Non-abusing parents whose child has been ill-treated by a trusted relative or friend can feel a serious loss of confidence about their own judgement. In cases of sexual abuse, for instance, a child can have been abused for some time and said nothing – or what s/he did say was not recognised as a serious cry for help. When the facts emerge, the non-abusing parent(s) are faced with a time of weeks, months, or even years, when their perception of events was completely wrong. This kind of discovery of abuse has been likened to bereavement or loss.
- A conflict of loyalties between the child and the alleged abuser, when this person is part of the family. Allegations of physical or sexual abuse can drive a wedge between members of a family, a situation which might never be resolved, even if the allegations turn out to be unfounded.
- Shame and embarrassment about what has happened and that their family life has, or will, become public. Once a child abuse investigation starts, professionals are obliged to ask many questions that intrude into what are otherwise private family matters.
- Distress and pressure from other family members, or local people who are not being supportive. Non-abusing parents may have to deal with relatives and neighbours who want to disbelieve the child, who blame the parent or who feel that the whole matter should have been dealt with by the family or immediate community.

You will support parents if you acknowledge their feelings and recognise the mixed and changing emotions. You are not saying that they are right to feel that way (for instance, in appearing to blame a child for keeping the abuse a secret) but you can show that you have heard what they said. You may be able to offer an alternative perspective, for example, by explaining why children can have such difficulty in telling.

You must also recognise that once an abuser has been removed from a family or denied any more access to a child, the situation does not suddenly go back to how it was before the crisis. The child may be distressed and have mixed feelings to deal with and so will the non-abusing adults of the family.

If parents are angry with you or with the centre as a whole, you again need to acknowledge that anger, rather than try to argue or get angry in return. There is no sure way to deal with anger and defuse the power of that emotion, but the following guidelines will help:

- Stay calm and do not respond to the parent's anger with your own anger or counter-claims that the parent is being unfair.
- Show that you recognise the parent's feelings. You are not saying s/he is right to be angry. Nor are you agreeing that his/her view is correct, that the centre is to blame or that all social workers are idiots.
- Listen to what the parent is saying – what has made him/her so angry? S/he may be expressing him/herself in a very emotional way, but can you work out the cause of the strong feelings?
- You can test the waters to see if the parent is ready to listen but it is unwise to push explanations or logic unless the parent seems receptive. You might say, 'I can see that you're angry. You feel the social worker won't answer your questions. Do you want me to explain what happens next?'
- Within the setting, you still have a responsibility for the children, who can become distressed and frightened by adults who appear out of control. A furious adult or one who is using violent or offensive language may need to be told firmly, 'I can see how angry you are, but I can't have you upsetting the children. I will talk with you outside the room.'
- All early years workers have a right to their own safety and any setting should have clear procedures on how staff come to a colleague's aid when an altercation gets out of hand.

Advice and information

Your aim is to share information appropriately with parents, so that they are aware of what is happening and feel more in control. Support them, but do not take over or carry out tasks that are their responsibility. It is not helpful to exclude them as this will make them feel that they have even less control over their family life than they already do.

THE STEPS IN THE CHILD PROTECTION PROCESS

If there is an investigation taking place, the parents of the child(ren) involved should be kept informed of what is happening in the process. The assigned social worker should be on hand to explain things to the parents, but they may prefer to talk to you, as somebody they knew before the crisis emerged. Make sure that you understand the child protection process, so that you can explain to parents what will happen next and that some events (for instance, taking children into care) are not inevitable. You can ensure that parents know about case conferences and their right to attend. Explain your role in such events and that although the parent may appreciate a friendly face, you have to give the centre's impartial report.

PARENTS AT CASE CONFERENCES

Normal practice is that parents are invited to case conferences about their children as part of the child protection process. Parents are not obliged to attend but there would have to be very good reasons for them to be excluded (see page 43).

Many professionals have been wary about the impact of parents attending case conferences. And certainly there was a time, before partnership with parents became an accepted aspect of good professional practice, when parents were not involved as a matter of course. Reviews of parental involvement in case conferences have raised a number of positive consequences although it is acknowledged that professionals may not always feel at ease.

The presence of parents forces professionals at a case conference to support their opinions properly. With parents watching and listening there is less likelihood of unsubstantiated opinions or offhand remarks about the family; discussion is likely to be more focused and objective. Conference members can listen to the parents and gain some understanding of how far they are likely to be motivated to take part in the treatment plan for this child, or to co-operate in any monitoring of the child's health or development.

It also allows parents to see the process for themselves and, at least sometimes, to reassure themselves that it is fair and that people are not condemning them out of hand. Parents are also able to see the different professionals working together.

In spite of the possible advantages of having parents at conferences, the focus must still be on the child's welfare. The professionals present, including any early years workers, have to be ready to express the more difficult issues about the child and family. As an early years worker who will give a report, you should not be making comments that will surprise and shock a parent because you should have had discussions regarding the relevant issues with the parent prior to the case conference. Nevertheless it can be hard for professionals to listen and appreciate parents' distress or fear about what is happening. You may be discomforted by an articulate defence by parents of their actions or a verbal attack about professional assumptions or attitudes.

SUPPORT FOR PARENTS IN CHILD CARE SKILLS

Parents whose abuse has arisen largely through ignorance of their child's basic needs may accept help within your setting. Children's and family centres are organised so that contracts can be made with parents for their attendance as well as that of their child. Other settings may not have the time and space to offer comprehensive work with parents. A setting has to look carefully as what can realistically be done, without reducing the quality of work with the children. One setting may be able to offer regular time, and support through discussion, to a parent, perhaps within an organised support group. Other settings cannot hope to organise this kind of work but can provide a friendly face, a listening ear and short conversations about children and ways of dealing with their needs.

Some parents may genuinely have very little idea about children's physical and emotional needs, possibly because the parents are very young themselves. Some adults have had disrupted childhoods, from which they have no useful memories of how to treat children well. In other families, serious stress may have overwhelmed the parents and caused them to neglect their children. Depending on other demands on your time and energy, you may be able to offer advice on some of the following:

- Basic child care such as food, clothing and hygiene. Any suggestions have to be realistic, given the parent's family circumstances and finances. In this area, as in any other aspect of child care, it will not help simply to suggest that parents follow the model established in your setting. Your centre is not a family home, let alone one under stress. If you have no experience of caring for children at home (whether your own or in work as a nanny), then talk with colleagues who can extend your understanding.
- Information on the usual range of development and behaviour of young children – for instance, that most two-year-olds do not do what they are told all the time. It is normal for children to want adults' attention and if they cannot get it easily, then they might become disruptive.

- Ideas on a positive approach to handling children's behaviour – for instance, being consistent, using encouragement and being willing to compromise. In this area, and any other aspect of children's lives, avoid implying that you always get things right or that there are definite answers. You should offer good ideas that are effective enough to make the effort to the parent worthwhile.
- Suggestions for how parents can enjoy being with their child(ren). You may have ideas on how they could play together, involve their child(ren) safely in domestic routine, watch a suitable television programme together or enjoy simple and free activities like going to the park, but again make sure that any suggestions can be sensibly incorporated into the parents' family life.

A consistent theme in this kind of help is encouraging parents to put their child's needs to the forefront of their lives. Keep realistic goals for your input and what parents can manage, learn and do, given their state of understanding and pressures. In the end they will choose whether to follow your ideas or specific advice and they need to feel that they are becoming more competent, rather than seeing you as the person with all the answers.

However hard the parents are trying, you must continue to monitor the child and your records of a child's development and behaviour will reflect any changes. You can still offer warmth and support to parents whilst maintaining that changes are necessary for the child's sake. You need, with support in your setting, to be impartial and objective about parents' behaviour with their children. You cannot remain neutral about children's welfare.

It is not your responsibility to try to make parents take advice or change negative patterns of behaviour with their children. The most important lesson for some parents is to learn that they are responsible for the consequences of their own actions and that they have to stop trying to shift the responsibility or blame onto other people.

SHARING IDEAS FOR THE CARE OF AN ABUSED CHILD

The confidence of non-abusing parents in their own skills can be severely shaken if abuse of their child(ren) comes to light. They may try to make everything up to the child with treats or abandon normal family ground rules. Or perhaps a parent feels that the child needs the security of positive family boundaries but is being overruled by someone else in the family. You may be able to help a parent in establishing flexible support for a child's distress which does not overturn previous ground rules. You may face similar problems in the centre, although this will not necessarily be the case as children react differently in the various settings of their young lives.

Listen to a parent's dilemma and, if it might help, explain how you are handling the child's behaviour in the centre. Describe how you affirm your care and liking of the child whilst being prepared to step in over disruptive or cruel behaviour to other children. Abused children can also become very quiet and inward-looking. Explain to the parent how you are giving time to the child, not trying to jolly her out of her feelings, but still encouraging any movement towards the way this child used to be.

A child who has been sexually abused may make inappropriate physical approaches to other children, or to workers. Parents may not realise that such consequences could follow from their child's experience. You can offer support by acknowledging the seriousness of this kind of behaviour, but explain that it is not unusual for sexually abused children. Explain to the parents how you are dealing with the behaviour.

Domestic Violence

In order to help parents, you have to have some understanding of the situation they are facing. The circumstances surrounding domestic violence are often very complex. People who have little experience of the problem often say, 'But surely, she could just leave', but women, or the smaller number of men, who are on the receiving end of domestic violence rarely have this option. Despite the violence, they may still be attached to their partner and hold on to the hope that s/he will change. They may excuse violent actions as the result of drink or stress, or feel that they in some way provoke the outbursts. It can be hard for parents to see similarities to a violent partner in the looks or behaviour of a loved child. Parents in violent homes are also often afraid that their children will be taken into care if the full extent of the violence emerges and so the violence remains as a family secret into which the children are drawn.

You may not be the person to help directly but you could be invaluable in alerting a parent to other sources of help and support. You may be able to boost a parent's confidence by reassuring him/her that s/he *is* able to help the children, when the failure to protect them from a violent partner may have seriously undermined this confidence.

Sometimes parents need to be alerted to the fact that the children are affected by violence in the home. Children can suffer serious emotional distress, even when they are not physically harmed. The parent may feel that s/he is protecting them, perhaps by tolerating the violence, and that the children are not really aware of what is happening. You may also support a parent who needs to be honest with the children about what is happening or if they all leave a violent parent. Another issue, relevant to the whole staff of a centre, is that children whose fathers are violent may desperately need models of caring and non-violent men. Such a positive image may be offered if you have male workers or volunteers in the centre.

Local and National Resources

No early years setting will ever provide all services for parents. Good practice in a centre is understanding what you can and should offer on site and keeping your knowledge up to date on what is available elsewhere. Unless you work in a specialist centre, it will not be appropriate to attempt to undertake direct work with parents on complex problems, such as severe depression or alcoholism.

You need to know, for instance, the kind of facilities available locally for women with post-natal depression. If you are working with a woman frightened by domestic violence, are there any local refuges to which she and her children could go? Where can someone go locally if they are addicted to alcohol, illegal or prescription drugs? Do local social services, or a voluntary organisation, offer respite care for a family overwhelmed by the needs of a severely disabled child or the care of an elderly relative?

The area in which you work may be well served, at least for some of these needs, or there may be very little to suggest. You need to remain realistic – offer the advice and information that you can; accept that you are not personally responsible for the shortcomings of any local services; and that it is not your job to push parents into using available units or advice groups.

ACTIVITY

All settings should keep a file, updated at regular intervals, with addresses, names and details of local services and special units. You can add national organisations who offer advice over telephone helplines or in practical publications. There are examples in this book on page 179.

If your setting does not have such a folder or file, then start one now. If one does already exist, then check that it is helpful for child protection issues as well as other aspects of early child care and education.

Support for workers

Supervision

Any staff working with a family, where there are allegations of child abuse, will be under some degree of stress. Early years settings should provide support, through discussions about the family and careful planning to guide a worker's approach.

- Supervision time should allow individual workers to express concerns, doubts or have a chance to explore aspects of the agreed approach that are uncertain or that involve new skills. Even experienced workers may welcome a chance to talk through how to handle a more difficult relationship with one or both parents or the best way forward with a child's disruptive pattern of behaviour.
- Workers have feelings and you may want to air your concern for the child and distress at what has happened. A professional approach to child protection includes an awareness of your feelings and taking opportunities to talk through them. It is not good practice to pretend that emotions have not been aroused by events.
- A senior worker should also help you to define your priorities. For instance, however sympathetic you may be to the dilemmas or stresses experienced by a parent, you need to maintain a strong focus on the child and his/her emotional and physical well-being.
- You may also welcome some guidance in managing your time. Depending on the kind of work you are expected to cover within the normal day, you may have to limit the amount of time you can offer to parents, and be clear about when you are available for conversation and when you are not.

Personal experience of abuse

A worker's own experience of abuse as a child or young person could be revived by working with an abused child and his/her family. As a senior worker you need to be aware that opening up the subject in your centre or sending workers on relevant courses may bring out staff's personal experiences, in one way or another.

Some early years workers, as with any other professionals, will have experienced such events in their personal lives. Indeed, people whose own lives have been relatively untroubled in the same way sometimes have difficulty in understanding the impact of stress and the struggle to cope with events that seem overwhelming. But all professionals have to weigh up:

- In what way their own difficult experiences (not just abuse) are relevant to their work.
- To what extent details are shared, with whom and when.
- How they seek support for unresolved problems or distress.

The personal experience of staff is as much an individual matter as children's experiences. What may help or be most appropriate for the worker on personal and professional levels will depend on the details of the situation:

- The current work may bring back memories and feelings that you believed you had resolved – what happened to you, or perhaps bad experiences of having tried to confide in someone when you were a child. This child's experience, or something that an adult has said, has brought back your own memories, as fresh as ever.
- If you never told anyone about the abuse you experienced, then working with this child or family may arouse strong, perhaps conflicting feelings about events which have so far remained private.
- It is possible that your memories are not of your own experience but that of someone close to you in childhood: a sibling or good friend, whose abusive experience touched you deeply as a child.

Good professional practice is to raise personal issues within supervision so that you can gain the support you need and seek a perspective that helps you to separate personal experience from how you work now with a child or family. Senior workers in any setting are responsible for giving time to staff and helping everyone involved to reach appropriate and supported decisions. The following points will help you whether you are offering supervision or are yourself working through memories of childhood abuse.

- Workers who themselves experienced childhood abuse should neither be regarded as too close to the topic to help a child, nor as the ideal key worker because of their own experience. There should not be an automatic decision in either direction.
- If your feelings about your own experience are still raw, especially if you have not disclosed your experience until this time, you may not be the best person to work with this child and family. It is not good practice in counselling on major crises such as bereavement or relationship breakdown to attempt to help others when your own feelings are currently in turmoil. It is often too difficult to unravel your own experiences from those of the person you are helping.
- If you have strong and unresolved feelings about your own abuse, then the professional course of action is to seek help. Your supervisor may be able to support you in your work, but will probably not be in a position to offer the time and expertise of concentrated counselling.

- If you were given support as a child and you have come to terms with the experience, then there is no reason why you should not be the key worker with this child and parent. It would be inappropriate to say, for instance, that a worker who lost a parent when young should not work with a bereaved child now. A similar line of argument has to be followed for workers who experienced childhood abuse, but whose feelings will not distort their current judgement.
- Use the opportunity of supervision to ensure that personal experiences are not over-influencing your judgement. For instance, perhaps you have unhappy memories of inappropriate touch when you were taken to bed with a parent or other relative. However, parents of children you know now may let wakeful children sleep with them or read them a story in bed on weekend mornings and nothing untoward has happened.

Supervision can be the best context for weighing up the personal and professional issues in a case, including whether a worker should share a personal experience of abuse with colleagues or parents.

- A worker should not be pushed into making a personal disclosure unless he or she is comfortable and wishes to do so. This guideline applies to any kind of personal experience in which strong feelings are also involved.
- The issues surrounding any disclosure of abuse should be discussed within supervision, especially if a less experienced worker is involved. S/he may not anticipate the possible consequences of sharing a highly personal experience.
- Workers also need to understand the place of any personal disclosure (not only abuse) in a helping relationship with a parent.

A worker with relevant personal experience may choose to mention this issue in discussion with colleagues. This might be in a situation such as a staff meeting in which some workers express persistent doubts that 'a respected person like the Reverend Mayfield could possibly hurt his own son' or workers cannot understand why a child has not previously told about persistent abuse. A worker with direct experience might decide to put the weight of that experience against colleagues' doubts or apparent inability to understand how young children can be intimidated, even if there is no threat of physical violence. If you choose to contribute your personal experience, you need to be prepared to give some details of your experience but you should not feel obligated to give a long and highly detailed account. In effect, you are saying to your colleagues, 'Respect my views on this. I know more than you do', so it is neither fair nor useful to limit yourself to,

'I was abused as a child but I don't want to talk about it. Just believe what I'm telling you.' However, after a few sentences of relevant explanation you could say, 'The rest is very personal and I don't want to say any more.'

Your colleagues will have mixed reactions, depending on exactly what you have shared. They may express sympathy, uneasiness or shock. Some colleagues may be curious and press for more details; some may react with comments like 'That didn't sound too bad, what's the fuss about?' It is possible that your disclosure may lead another colleague to share unhappy childhood experiences.

You have chosen to bring something personal into a more public arena, but it is still fair of you to ask colleagues not to repeat what you said outside the staff group.

You need to consider carefully, and discuss with your supervisor, the circumstances under which a personal experience of abuse should be shared with parents. Generally speaking, you should have a sound reason for sharing any personal experience with parents, such as helping them to find another perspective, to reassure them that such events happen to other 'normal' people or to help them gain insight into how the child may be feeling. It should be an active decision, rather than sharing without thinking about the consequences. In a helping relationship with parents (for any problem they are experiencing), personal disclosures need to be used positively.

Your experience may provide a valuable perspective but it does not make you an expert on this child's experience. You may understand how this child *might* be feeling, but you do not know. Any discussions about possible action must focus on the individual child and family. Do not be tempted towards a particular course of action because it helped you as a child, or because you wish somebody had taken this approach for you.

Discussion of your experience should be brief; the aim of your disclosure is to help the parent, not to gain time for you to talk or to work through unresolved issues. The focus of the discussion should remain on the issue in hand; parents should not become preoccupied with your problems.

Allegations against staff

Much of this chapter has approached child protection from the perspective that risk to the child comes from outside the early years setting. However, there have been reminders that allegations may be made against staff and this section directly addresses this topic.

All early years settings, led by the head of centre, have to be seen to take a serious view of any allegations, by parents, children or colleagues, about the behaviour of paid workers, volunteers or visitors to the centre. Most of the information and guidelines given in other sections of this book are equally relevant when people internal to your setting are involved. Remember to:

- Listen carefully to what you are told, whether you are a worker listening to a child or parent, or you are a senior member of staff listening to the concerns of another worker.
- Gather your information but do not leap to conclusions one way or another. You should discuss the matter with the worker or the volunteer in question. At this stage, you may not have to name the source of your concern, although the worker may know, or have an idea, who has raised the concern about his/her practice.
- Make accurate notes following all the guidelines for good practice from page 103.
- Discuss the matter with appropriate people more senior to yourself or in a position to help you establish a sound perspective on the matter. A worker should speak with a senior or the head of centre. If you are the head of centre then you might talk with the local Under-Eights Advisor, your line manager, the chair of your centre's management committee or another appropriate professional with whom you can speak in confidence.
- Follow the procedures set out by your centre and ensure that anyone involved – parent(s), workers and other professionals – realises that you are acting in accordance with previously agreed guidelines.

There may be an acceptable and credible explanation for the concern that has been raised about a worker's behaviour. This explanation should be entered into the written record in the same way as would a parent's account of a child's injury, when it is judged that the matter has been satisfactorily explained.

You might be reassured that child abuse has not occurred, but more general issues of good practice might have been highlighted by the incident. Senior workers should address relevant issues sooner rather than later, either through supervision or broader staff discussion if appropriate. A worker may have been lax in informing parents about troublesome incidents between children in the centre or failed to mention a child's accident. Perhaps nobody checked that this parent's permission had been obtained for local trips out of the nursery. Or a parent's complaint might bring to light that a worker does personal shopping on trips out with children and then drops into her home on the way back to the centre. Alternatively, a parent's concern might make the centre re-assess an inappropriately open-door policy about visitors to the setting or a large rota of volunteers who are barely checked.

If there is clear evidence or serious reason to suspect physical or sexual abuse, then procedures for dealing with an accused worker would follow those used for dealing with any adult. Depending on the severity of the accusations, a worker would almost certainly be suspended whilst further enquiries were undertaken.

When there are allegations of child abuse within an early years setting, feelings can run high. Workers may find the allegations hard to believe – and everyone has to remember that suspicions may be unfounded. Alternatively, some workers may be distressed or self-critical because they did not take their uneasiness about someone more seriously. Support will be needed from within the setting and from appropriate sources within the wider local early years network.

Allegations of neglect or emotional abuse are always harder to prove, or disprove. However, observations of a worker or volunteer may be sufficient to question the quality of their practice, even if establishing child abuse is not a likely possibility. Perhaps a worker has developed bad habits of shouting at children, nagging or ridiculing them for their mistakes. Such bad practice should be handled through supervision and workers given very clear directions about appropriate behaviour with children. Workers also need to be firmly warned if their behaviour suggests that they have favourites among the children or their reactions to children are coloured by poor relationships with their parents. Your setting should have clear policies about issues such as a positive approach to children's behaviour and bad practice can be related to the expectations made clear in everyone's job description.

Discussions with workers within supervision regarding bad practice should be recorded in specific terms in the workers' files. When a worker's behaviour has been called into question, the actions taken should not remain an internal matter between the worker and the head of centre – other appropriate people should be informed and consulted. Depending on exactly how your centre is organised, you might contact your line manager, the chair of the centre management committee or the Under-Eights Advisor. If a worker does not heed warnings and persists in bad practice then s/he might eventually be dismissed. However, proper procedures must be followed to avoid accusations of wrongful dismissal. A senior worker may, for instance, have to ensure that a certain number of clear verbal and written warnings have been given to a worker. Check your own procedures; they will be relevant whether or not the bad practice in question is alleged child abuse.

Communication with children and parents

In addition to supportive work with the children directly involved, there should also be communication with parents and probably with the other children in the setting. The head of centre, in collaboration with the line manager, management committee or other appropriate group should make specific plans that can be shared with the whole staff group. The best approach will depend on what has happened, how far parents were involved in bringing abuse or ill-treatment to light and the age of the children.

When children have been ill-treated by workers or volunteers it is important that their experience is recognised. They need to know that responsible adults have taken notice and action on the children's behalf. Depending on what has happened, the children might be reassured that the behaviour of a volunteer was wrong and this person will not be allowed to come to the centre anymore. If there has been long-term or organised abuse in a setting, children may need specialist help supported by the care of workers whom they know and who were not involved. Children need to be reassured that they, or their peers, have been tricked by adults whose behaviour was wrong.

A setting should be ready to talk to parents or to deal properly with questions that parents ask. The local parent grapevine will operate with speed and the only way to increase the chances that accurate information is being passed around is to make that information available. In the early stage of an investigation workers might be told to say that complaints about a named worker or volunteer are being taken seriously and thoroughly checked. At this time it is important that staff do not allow themselves to be drawn into gossip. An agreement reached in a staff meeting might be that further questions by concerned parents are deflected courteously with a reply such as, 'I honestly don't know any more details. It's very important that we all keep an open mind for the moment. Miriam [centre manager] will send a letter to everyone when we know what's happening.' If a worker is dismissed then it is sensible to give an explanation to the parents, who will otherwise speculate about the reasons. The head of centre should consult the management committee, or other line management, about how best to phrase any communication, whether spoken or written.

Case Study

A class of seven-year-olds was supervised by a supply teacher for two days when their own teacher was sick. The supply teacher was unable to control the class and, although the children were initially amused by the chaos, they became increasingly distressed by the teacher's screaming and odd behaviour. Two children who played up were chased out of the classroom and around the playground, leaving the main group alone. The teacher got into a wrestling match with one child over a book when the child would not let go. Then on the second day, the same child was slapped twice on the hands for being cheeky.

On the third day the class's own teacher returned and pieced together what had happened from what some of the children told her and reports from colleagues who had heard the screaming. With the support of the head, the teacher first spoke to the whole class explaining that she was concerned about how the supply teacher seemed to have behaved with the class and needed to find out exactly what had happened. She reassured the class that she was not trying to blame them – it was clear from some children's comments that they were expecting to be criticised for having misbehaved with the supply teacher. The class teacher and the head spoke individually with each child in the class to build up an accurate picture of what had happened. They were then able to say to the whole class the next day that the supply teacher had behaved badly. No teacher was allowed to hit children, this person would never be allowed back into the school again and they would be sending a report on what she had done.

QUESTIONS

1. In this case, the head decided not to write to parents over the incident. What do you think of this decision? If you think she should have sent a letter, what are your reasons?
2. What does the example illustrate about children's expectations of adults?

Child abuse and the courts

Generally speaking, all the professionals involved in a child protection case will work to achieve an agreement on what should happen for the welfare of the child(ren) without going to court. If a parent, or other relevant carer, is clearly taking effective steps to protect the child and accepting the help that is on offer, then the courts will not be involved. The Children Act 1989 established that orders, or other kinds of legal intervention, should not be pursued in child protection cases, unless there is evidence that such steps are in the best interests of the child(ren).

However, it is possible that a child abuse case in which you are the involved worker could go to court. The social worker in charge of the case might seek a specific order in relation to the case, and your input in discussions with the social worker might have been important in supporting their decision that an order was necessary for the well-being of the child.

Civil proceedings

Civil courts are less formal than criminal courts and the standard of proof is different. In civil proceedings for child protection, there has to be evidence that suggests **on the balance of probabilities** that a child has been abused and that a named person (or persons) is the likely abuser. In criminal proceedings the evidence has to be **beyond reasonable doubt** – a tougher test of any evidence.

Civil proceedings in court can lead to rulings that the named alleged abuser stays away from the child or can only have supervised contact. A social worker might be involved in such contact or some arrangement might be made with your own early years setting. Alternatively, a ruling might be made that the child should be removed from the family home as the only way to ensure his/her safety. Foster parents or the staff of a residential children's home might then supervise the agreed contact. Civil proceedings allow for a range of steps to protect the child(ren) but do not involve any prosecution against the alleged abuser(s).

Civil proceedings are not only less formal but tend to be less confrontational than the legal process in a criminal court. But there can still be disagreements and arguments. If an acceptable solution has been agreed between social workers and the family, the case can be resolved outside the courtroom. Civil proceedings are more likely to occur when:

- The local authority social workers cannot reach an agreement with the family about what has happened, or is continuing to happen, to the child, or about the family's response to the situation.
- The child protection team judges that children need to be removed from the family and no voluntary arrangement has successfully been agreed with the parents or other relatives.
- Custody and access issues in a matrimonial dispute hinge on an allegation of abuse.

Children do not have to appear in civil proceedings, whereas a child may be called as a witness for the prosecution in a criminal case (see page 146). Children in civil proceedings have an independent legal representative, different from the solicitor for the local authority, and another solicitor represents the parent(s). The court also appoints a guardian *ad litem* (GAL), who will continue to represent the child's best interests and wishes after the case leaves court. GALs are advocates on behalf of the child.

It is possible that early years workers might be called to civil proceedings to give evidence about a child. You might have knowledge and records of a child's physical health, development or behaviour that have a bearing on the child's need for protection. You may have observed important incidents between a parent and child, or the child may have chosen to disclose an experience of abuse to you. The procedure in civil courts is not as adversarial as in criminal proceedings, but the key issues about being a reliable and credible witness are equally important.

In most instances, it is very difficult to prove beyond reasonable doubt that sexual abuse, in particular, has taken place, or prove the identity of the abuser. So most cases of sexual abuse that reach a court are heard in civil and not criminal courts.

Criminal proceedings

Only a minority of child abuse cases reach the courts as part of criminal proceedings. A prosecution will only be undertaken when the abuse, if proven, falls into the category of a crime and the Crown Prosecution Service judges that there is sufficient evidence to support the case (see also page 40 about the role of the police).

If you are called as a witness

Most readers of this book will not experience being a witness in civil or criminal proceedings for alleged child abuse. It is not a frequent event, but it could happen, especially if you work in a children's or family centre that offers a service to families under stress.

Being a witness can be an uncomfortable, even daunting, experience, particularly in criminal proceedings. An understanding of the process and your role can help to prepare you for going to court.

- Before the day of the court hearing, the local authority lawyer should allow time to meet you. S/he will explain what will happen and go through any practical issues about your evidence. The lawyer will alert you to the kind of questions that s/he will ask you as the case is developed. The lawyer may also be able to guess what questions are likely to be put to you by the defence lawyer. If you have any uncertainty or new information, speak up now. Lawyers' nightmares are composed of court scenes in which their witness suddenly reveals new facts or voices doubts.
- If there seems to be a delay in your being contacted, then phone the local authority lawyer yourself, especially if this is your first time as a witness. You might also welcome a prior visit to the court room, if possible, so that you know in advance the general layout of the room. Unless you have experience of a court room, for instance through jury service, you may have very little idea of what to expect.
- On the day, dress appropriately in smart clothes. Do not dress casually, even if jeans and sweatshirts are usual for your place of work.
- Arrive at the court with time to spare so that you do not feel rushed.

Once you are in the witness box there are some practical guidelines to bear in mind:

- Speak steadily and clearly. Look up and not down at the floor. Although you are asked the questions by the lawyer, you should direct your reply to the magistrate or judge sitting at the bench. This style can feel strange at first but you will soon become accustomed to it.
- You probably need to talk at slightly slower than normal conversational pace. The clerk of the court will be taking notes and magistrates or judges usually take their own notes as well.
- If you could not hear all or part of a question, ask for it to be repeated. If you do not understand the question, then say so.

- Witnesses are not expected to remember everything by heart when they are going to be asked for many details, as you could be. It is acceptable for you to take notes into the witness box and to consult them to ensure the accuracy of your answers, for instance about dates or what a child said. But, as soon as you use notes as a witness you can legitimately be asked when you wrote up your notes – the point about the timeliness of recording is also made on page 108. Your notes can also be taken in as evidence and made available to the defence lawyer in criminal proceedings.
- Your evidence should be limited to what you personally observed, what you can honestly say 'I saw' or 'I heard'. Quote a parent's or child's actual words only if you are certain that those were the exact words used. Otherwise, just give the gist of what was said.
- Answer the question and do not move on to other topics unless what you have to say is a relevant explanation. You would normally reply more than 'Yes' or 'No' to a question, although there may be instances when this simple answer is appropriate.
- In some cases your evidence may include positive points about a parent. Express these as honestly as any negative evidence.
- Part of your legitimate evidence may be second-hand, in that you were told something by another person. Express this accurately: for example, 'Mrs Jones asked to speak with me on the 25th of May. She told me she had seen Selina's mother hit the child and Selina had fallen against the concrete post.' You know what you were told, but you do not know from your own direct observation that Selina was hit by her mother.
- You may be asked to express an opinion based on your knowledge of the child or of children in general. Support your opinion with 'because . . .' or 'my experience has been . . .' Do not go beyond issues on which you can reasonably express an opinion. Other people in court will not necessarily be experienced with children, so be ready to explain any specialist terms or preferably use ordinary language. The local authority lawyer should be ready to help you prepare for this.
- If you do not know the answer to a question, then it is better to say, 'I don't know' or perhaps something like 'I wasn't able to hear what Samantha's father said to her. I could see that Samantha was crying and pulling away from her father.'

In criminal proceedings, witnesses are first questioned by the prosecution lawyer. There should be no surprises in this part of your evidence, since your answers are part of the local authority or the police case. You will then be cross-examined by the defence lawyer. In civil proceedings the parents' lawyer may ask you questions.

The job of defence lawyers is to defend their clients, so their responsibility is to cast doubt on the evidence. Lawyers use a number of tactics in order to achieve this aim. The result for witnesses can be anything from slightly to highly uncomfortable. Defence lawyers are not being personally unpleasant to you in doubting your observations or experience; they are simply doing their job. You should remain focused and calm. Avoid getting either annoyed or upset. Do not relax, even if the approach is initially friendly. You are not having an informal conversation, the defence lawyer is cross-questioning you on behalf of the accused.

If you are called as a witness, it is unlikely that all the practical issues about evidence outlined in this section will arise, but some of them will be part of your court experience. Be prepared and remember that your time in court is a particular kind of exchange. Concentrate on the task in hand and do not relax until you have left the witness box.

This section assumes you will be called as a witness for the prosecution. It is possible you may be called by the defence team. Most of the practical points are still relevant; certainly do not be tempted to go beyond what you know, however much you like a parent.

Children as witnesses

During the 1990s, attitudes and procedures regarding children appearing as witnesses in abuse cases within criminal proceedings have changed. The evidence of children has become more acceptable, partly as a general recognition in child protection that children can understand the difference between truth and lies. However, prosecutions are often not pursued when the children are young, especially if under the age of seven. If the alleged abuser pleads 'guilty', then children do not have to go to court, but if s/he pleads 'not guilty', then children's evidence has to be heard in court and they have to undergo cross-examination. Children are in a particularly vulnerable position over allegations of sexual abuse as the child's evidence may be the main or only strand of the prosecution's case.

Apart from considerations of the weight of the evidence, police and social workers are also concerned about a child's well-being. They have to make a balanced decision on whether a child should appear as a witness by weighing up the likely distress to the child against the wish to see an alleged abuser appropriately punished in law. The court process in a prosecution is confrontational and can be distressing for any witness, let alone young children. The defendant must be presumed innocent until proven guilty and it is the job of the defence lawyer to question and undermine the evidence against his/her client, whether this is provided by an adult or a child.

There are strict guidelines which govern how children give evidence in order to reduce the likely distress of the experience:

- Children can be interviewed for their evidence before the court hearing. The child is interviewed in a special police suite which looks like a living room and the whole interview is video recorded. This means that children do not have to repeat their evidence for the prosecution case. The tape is played to the court.
- No interview should be longer than an hour. Children can be interviewed more than once, in separate sessions, but not too many times.
- Children must not be prepared for the interview and there must be no leading questions from the adult. In other words, there must be reassurance that children's evidence has not been shaped by adult questioning.
- A video link between the court room and a separate room can be used so that children do not have to be in court, and do not have to face their alleged abuser. Alternatively, some courtrooms have a screen that shields the child or young person from the majority of the court. Children will still be cross-examined by the defence lawyer, via the video link, and have to answer questions about their evidence. In sexual abuse cases particularly, children and young people can find this experience embarrassing and intimidating. The main thrust of the defence is also likely to be that the child witness is lying or, at the very least, confused and mistaken.
- Police officers and social workers have to weigh up whether individual children will be able to cope with cross-examination and their possible distress at having their word doubted in public. The non-abusing parents also have to consider these difficult issues on their child's behalf.

The social worker and police child protection specialist will prepare a child for the experience of being in court (but not for the interview). As an early years worker closely involved with the family, you could also have an important role in supporting the child and parent(s) and helping them to have realistic expectations of what may happen.

6

Good Practice with Children

There are many aspects of good practice with young children and their families that will support your approach to child protection. These ways of working will be positive for children and should be in place regardless of whether your setting ever has concerns over abuse. Good practice in observation and record keeping is discussed in Chapter 4 and partnership with parents is raised in many places in the book. The good practice issues described in this chapter will help children develop respect for themselves and build an image of how adults ought to behave.

The physical care of children

The value of good physical care

Physical care is an important means of communication with young children and can be a powerful vehicle in their learning about adults and themselves. Tradition in early years has mistakenly undervalued the contribution of care, seeing it as the poor relation to education. Sometimes this attitude still prevails and this can be a major stumbling block to quality in early years settings.

Appropriate physical care routines give children an experience of individual attention and appropriate, affectionate touch. Good experience of physical care can help children to build a positive image of how adults behave properly towards children. It is important to treat babies and young children with respect in their physical care – they care about how they are handled and notice the difference.

Say What You Are Doing

Babies and toddlers should be treated with respect and not simply lifted up swiftly or bundled off to be changed without thought for their feelings. It only takes additional seconds to smile or say 'hello' to a baby or toddler and perhaps to follow up with 'Josh, it's time to change you' or 'Hello, Nneka. How about cheese and mash for lunch?' This effort is time and attention very well spent, since the young child feels involved, rather than a small, immobile person to whom other people do things when it suits them.

Babies and toddlers should not be treated like a bag of dirty washing or a body to be fed. Thoughtless routines, or a setting that undervalues care, can effectively put babies and toddlers on a conveyer belt between workers who are more interested in talking to each other than to the children. Workers may not intend to distress the young children but this can be the result.

Personal Communication

Changing time for a baby or toddler should be a personal time when the adult talks with the baby and listens to what s/he says in reply, even if there are no real words yet. The early years worker (parent or any other carer) can tune into the baby's mood, offering a song or a verbal ritual that the baby comes to recognise (such as tuneful patterns like 'Hup, one, two, three!'). Workers can acknowledge a baby's fretful mood by talking reassuringly to a baby who does not feel like being changed.

The key worker system allows children to learn the ways of individual adults and, in turn, the adult (key worker) can tune into the temperament and likes and dislikes of the child. Young children should not be taught that, when you are a child, any adult can appear and deal with your intimate physical needs, regardless of whether you like them or know them well.

Share the Care with Children

Toddlers want to help with their dressing and mealtimes. Again, a timing of the care routines adjusted to the children, rather than adult convenience, will support young children to feel competent and yet able to ask for help. Young children need to feel that their growing abilities are respected and appreciated, but that being able to do something for yourself does not mean that adult support is withdrawn.

Tell children what you are doing and, where appropriate, ask if they want some help rather than pushing assistance upon them. Show them how to care for themselves and encourage them in all their efforts. Avoid swooping in without words to wipe a nose or a bottom, or to push children's arms into their coat when they are almost there through their own ability.

Show Respect for Young Children

Young children need a great deal of physically intimate care but this can be offered with respect.

Some young children are happy to sit on a pot, or on the toilet with the door open, and hold a conversation with a worker or their friends. Other

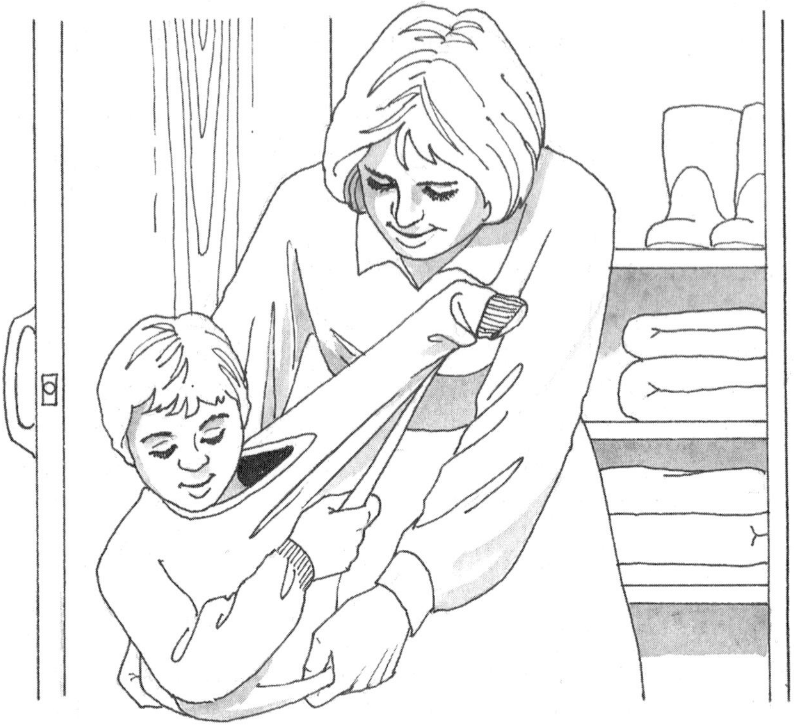

Helping young children to feel competent

children, sometimes from a very young age, want more privacy. Their wish should be respected and can be met along with any concerns about safety. For instance, in your setting the judgement may be that it is unsafe to have locks on the toilet doors. But you can still establish a tradition of respectful behaviour by allowing children to shut the door and informing adults and other children that they should not go barging in without knocking.

Some children are content to strip down to their underwear for games or dance in the early years of school, but others feel uncomfortable doing this and there should always be an alternative offered to parents before children are faced with the situation. Children may simply not want to run about in their knickers and vest. Adults also spend energy under other circumstances explaining to young children that they should not flip up their skirt or pull their trousers down in public! Children who have health conditions that affect their skin, such as eczema, can be very self-conscious about exposing their limbs. They may fear, with some justification, that other children will tease them. Some families will have religious reasons for not wanting their children to undress for games.

Disabled Children

All the above points are also important in the care of disabled children. They may be unable to deal with their own needs at an age when their peers are managing with little or no help. Physical limitations may hinder children's persistent efforts to take on their own care or mean that they need plenty of time and therefore patience and appreciation from their carer. Children with severe learning disabilities may take time to understand what they need to do, or to follow a sequence in their own physical care.

Any setting with disabled children needs high standards in care and the behaviour of the adult carers. Otherwise children can be at a greater risk of abuse because they might build an image of themselves as people upon whom a range of adults impose physically intimate procedures, whether the child wants it or not (see page 27).

Case Study

Even very young children have a sense of bodily dignity and can be distressed and outraged by careless treatment. One example was recounted to me by the mother of two-year-old Alice. The little girl had a persistent attack of vaginal thrush and her mother took Alice to the local health clinic. They were left to wait a considerable time in an examining room and then a male doctor, whom they had not met before, came in at speed. He approached Alice, who was lying on the bed and, without any words, pulled down her knickers and pushed her legs apart to look at the inflamed area. With a few words to Alice's mother the doctor confirmed it was thrush, wrote a prescription and left. Alice was in tears and spoke over the following days about 'the nasty man'.

Alice's mother comforted her at the time and realised that Alice's upset was spreading to any male doctor. On their next visit to the clinic, the usual male doctor in the practice was seeing patients. Alice's mother explained the situation and said that Alice was clear that she wanted to be examined by a 'lady'. Fortunately this doctor took the view that Alice's preference was understandable, that he would respect a woman's wish to see a female doctor and Alice's views counted just as much. He phoned through to a female colleague who examined Alice.

QUESTIONS

1 It was fortunate that Alice's next trip to the health clinic was so much better handled. What do you think could have been the consequences for Alice's feelings if she had experienced disrespect yet again?

2 Collect examples of good practice in treatment of young children. In what ways do respectful adults behave towards children during their health care or when the child's experience could be embarrassing, uncomfortable or painful?

Affection and physical contact

Physical – not sexual – contact

Children are very physical beings: they learn a great deal through their senses. But there is a difference between physicality and sexuality. The confusion between these two concepts arises mainly from the wide influence of Sigmund Freud's claims about the sexual basis to children's development (through a young child's supposedly powerful feelings of attraction to the parent of the opposite sex and jealousy of the parent of the same sex). But infantile sexuality is an idea, not a fact, and several respected theorists following Freud in the psychodynamic tradition disagreed strongly with his emphasis on sexuality in childhood.

Many young children are temporarily interested in their own or their peers' private parts but this does not make them sexual in the adult sense. Their curiosity has to be seen in the context of their general fascination with the unknown or unexplained – especially if adults indicate that they do not want children to explore in this way. In the family home, children spend a lot of time trying to post small objects into the video, emptying out drawers and waste bins or playing with saucepans – such behaviour is not proof that children are obsessed with rubbish or metal objects.

Children's emotional needs

Children need warmth, expressed affection and physical closeness, but there is an enormous gap between responding to children's need for closeness and wishing to abuse them. There has been so much publicity about sexual abuse that some parents and early years workers have become concerned that their appropriate affection for children is open to misinterpretation. Yet the majority of adults do not want and will never want to abuse children sexually. It will be nothing short of a tragedy for children if their need for physical closeness and communication is denied because adults fear they may be wrongly accused of abuse.

Children need experience of touch, of respectful contact. This helps them to form a psychologically healthy framework in which to judge adult behaviour, or the actions of older children and teenagers. Children need to be able to make some sense of people who are not behaving properly towards them, who require affection or who are imposing their own views and needs on them. They have to build from their own experience the confidence to believe that 'this doesn't feel right' or to say 'I don't want this and I can say "no".'

Children with no experience of appropriate, close physical affection can be dangerously vulnerable to adults who wish to abuse them sexually (and often use as an excuse the claim that children have a sexual nature). Emotionally deprived children are at risk for two reasons:

- They can be desperate for affection and are willing to accept it from any adult who appears to like them and be willing to pay them some attention.
- They have no comparison point for judging the behaviour of an adult who starts to impose upon them.

The points in this chapter apply to all workers – both female and male. Children will not be effectively protected if they are kept away from men, if the male workers of a team are excluded from the more personal care routines or if male workers are banned from normal close contact with children. Children need experience of appropriate caring behaviour from both sexes. All early years settings need to have staff discussions about this issue and to avoid any naïve reliance on the restriction of male workers in the team (see page 62).

All workers and volunteers should be guided by children in expressions of affection. It is inappropriate for adults to demand expressions of affection or particular kinds of expression, such as being kissed or hugged, if a child does not spontaneously offer. Nor is it reasonable for workers to want affection from a baby or child in order to cheer themselves up.

Children vary: some like to sit close, to hold hands or to sit on a worker's lap, but others are more reserved. There is not necessarily any cause to worry about the less demonstrative children. They may be less affectionate by temperament or their family style may be warm, but not physically demonstrative. There is no need to be concerned about reserved children unless other behaviour from them makes you wonder if they are wary of adults to the point of being afraid. In a similar way you need not worry about very affectionate children, unless they are indiscriminate in their affections. You might worry about some particular expressions of affection, such as open-mouthed kissing or rubbing against workers' private parts.

Children's curiosity

An appropriate adult role needs to be based on knowledge of children's usual development:

- Be ready to answer children's questions about how bodies work. Give simple, honest answers and see if the child requests further information. No child wants to hear absolutely everything you know about digestion or reproduction in response to their first question. Some children do not ask many questions of this kind; some are fascinated.
- Caring adults have a responsibility to help children learn about appropriate boundaries for behaviour. You will be communicating to children what is usual public behaviour and what should be more private.
- You will also, where necessary, be explaining to children about private areas of people's bodies and their right to refuse being touched or examined where they do not wish. Most children are able to learn the distinctions and their curious explorations do not get to extreme levels.
- If you work with older, or very articulate, children, there may be questions that you feel parents should handle. Perhaps a child has heard an item of news about a sexual scandal and asks you detailed questions. You could say, 'That's a good question, but I think your parents should answer that.' And if the child reasonably asks, 'Why?', you can say, 'Mums and Dads often have strong feelings about what their children should be told on this subject. It's not for me to decide what to tell you.' Make sure that you speak with the child's parents later that day. Reassure them that you feel their son or daughter asked a fair question, but one that they should answer in their own way. It is courteous to raise the issue of how you answer such questions with the parents. If you do answer any questions you should tell the parent(s) how you answered them on this occasion and whether they would rather you handled the topic differently next time.

Communication with children

Children are supported by positive experiences of adults who listen to their views, questions and worries. Children who feel they can turn to an adult who will take them seriously is far more likely to speak up about an experience that is causing them concern or unease, but might not necessarily be abusive. Children who have experienced respectful communication from adults are also likely to believe that what they feel and think matters and should not be ignored by any adults for their own ends.

Good habits in communication

Children will be helped in your setting by adults who give them time and attention.

- Make a habit of listening to what children want to say to you and watch what their body language tells you as well as listening to their words.
- Avoid assuming that, as an adult, you know what a child is thinking or should be thinking or feeling. Ask them what they are thinking and feeling and listen fully to their replies.
- Be ready to take children seriously – their feelings, worries, confusions, or dislikes about people. You should not agree that their fears are necessarily justified or feed their worries, but you should take their views seriously, reassure them where appropriate and take further action or investigation if it seems necessary.
- Respect children's concerns and physical feelings. Children feel dismissed and belittled by remarks such as, 'You don't really feel like that' or 'You're making a fuss, that doesn't hurt.'
- Help children to learn respectful communication with each other: listening, not interrupting and taking someone else's view into account.
- Answer children's questions honestly, even if you find some topics slightly embarrassing, or refer them to their parents (see the previous section).

Dealing with emotions

Adult Reactions

Children are learning a great deal about feelings: their own, the feelings of others and the general ground rules for dealing with feelings. Even if adults do not believe that they are giving specific messages about emotions, their views emerge through their behaviour. For example, a worker (or parent) might react differently to a girl who is crying than to a boy of the same age who is crying. A brusque reaction, or even a preference for jollying children out of deep feelings, can tell the child that this adult, and perhaps others too, do not want to hear and see that s/he is upset, frightened or worried.

Some adults, workers and parents seem to be resistant to accepting that young children have strong feelings: that they can be emotionally hurt by how they are treated and do not just snap out of sadness or forget all about unhappy events. This might be due to the following:

- Sometimes adults resist taking the child's perspective. The adult judgement about a situation prevails so that s/he says, 'That's not worth making a fuss about' or even 'You're not hurt that badly.' The same, insensitive adults sometimes make offhand remarks about children within their hearing, as if the children will not overhear or will not care about comments that would annoy the adults themselves.
- Possibly, some adults find it less trouble to believe that young children are incapable of serious distress, that they 'don't really notice' or that 'young children soon get over upsets.' The advantage to adults of this convenient, and inaccurate, view is that they can avoid any feelings of responsibility to support distressed children. Young children get over upsets when adults offer swift and appropriate support.
- Adults may also try to protect themselves against their own possible distress when children are unhappy. This is one explanation of the view that a child was not 'really upset' at the beginning of the session, because s/he cheered up later. Some adults also challenge the genuineness of children's upset on the grounds that there are no 'real tears'.

Positive Support for Children

A far more positive approach is to accept children's feelings as they are expressed to you. You need to tune in to the seriousness as expressed by the child – neither belittling his strong feelings nor making more of an incident than he wants. You can support children in recognising and dealing with their feelings through how you talk and listen to them.

You can also show children ways of expressing feelings by how you handle your own emotions – in words and actions. For instance:

- You might agree with children – 'I'm sad about Minnie [the nursery mouse who died] too. I miss her little face in the morning.' Or you might admit that you too are touched by a children's film or video – 'Yes, I know it's just a story. But that doesn't stop me feeling a bit sad.'
- You can show feelings of happiness and elation in shared activities with children – 'We did it! We made it work. I'm so proud of us all.'
- Sometimes the emotion may be frustration or disappointment – 'That is so annoying. There's something the matter with this glue. Let me see if I've got something that will work.'

- You will also get opportunities to show children assertive, rather than aggressive, behaviour – 'Yes, I thought that man in the market was very rude to us. I told him so, but I wasn't going to shout the way that he did.'

Group Work with Children

Very young children need individual attention and will not respond well to being treated as one of a group, but three- and four-year-olds are more able to operate both as individuals and as members of their nursery or preschool group. Opportunities will arise for exploring feelings within the different play activities in your setting. For instance:

- Feelings and dilemmas often feature in books that you read to a small group or at storytelling time. The worry or fear experienced by a character in a story can be a good opportunity to discuss feelings with children. You might talk a little about what the children think a character may be feeling, or what they might feel in the same situation. A happy resolution to the story might lead to discussion from the children about what makes them happy or excited.

Storytelling might provoke discussion about feelings

- A regular circle time with a small group can be a chance for individual children, if they wish, to share something that has happened in their life. On occasion children may tell about events that provoke sympathy, for instance, that Grandma has gone into hospital or that their rabbit has died. At other times, children may share happy events, for instance, that they have a new baby sister and Mum lets them help care for her.
- Pretend play in the home corner or with dolls can be a way to explore feelings as well as try out skills that a child might not be allowed to practise in a real kitchen or with a real baby. Children's mixed feelings can emerge through play with puppets or dolls and can provide a relief for frustrations in their lives which are not necessarily abusive experiences.

It is good practice to use these play and group methods alongside being available to listen to children. Never think of books or puppets as a substitute for caring adult communication with individual children.

ACTIVITY

Gather ideas and examples of how you can support children's feelings in a positive way in your setting.

1. Note down examples of play or small group discussion. What have you done within the last fortnight with the children? What emerged from the play or the group conversation? What seemed to interest the children most?
2. Look out for the opportunities that you provide for children to talk with you on a one-to-one basis. Perhaps keep a note, over a fortnight, of conversations that you have with children, when the child has wanted to share something with you. How far are you able, honestly, to give the time individual children would like? Are there any implications for how you organise the day, or session, or make yourself available to the children?

A positive policy for dealing with children's behaviour

Children need experience of adults who handle their behaviour in a positive way, without using threats, verbal humiliation or physical forms of intimidation or punishment. Your setting should have a clear policy on how you deal with children's behaviour and the ideas and approaches should be shared with parents. Some families will be pleased to hear that you act in the same way that they do at home; others may be confused and need reassurance that removing physical forms of punishment definitely does not mean that you let the children run wild.

A positive approach to children

The main themes of a positive approach are as follows:

- You should look at things, at least sometimes, from the children's perspective – through their eyes. Children are helped to behave well and to deal with their feelings or frustrations by adults who allow for children's understanding and do not simply impose adult views.
- Workers and parents need to be clear about what they want children to do, and not just what they *do not* want them to do. You can communicate and explain clear ground rules to children, phrased as 'Please do . . .' and not as a list of 'don'ts'.
- Follow your own ground rules and show positive behaviour yourself children are never impressed by the approach of 'Never mind how I behave. Just do what I tell you!' Children are helped and inspired by adults who model what they would like children to do: helping others, saying 'sorry' and dealing with frustrations in ways that do not impose on other people.
- Encourage and show pleasure in the behaviour that you want from children. Notice by smiles and words when they have made an effort. You do not have to reward children with treats or lavish praise. In fact, overdoing reward can backfire, because children then expect to be rewarded with sweets or privileges all the time.
- Be generous with your time and energy in giving children encouragement for what has been well done. Avoid putting most of your efforts into catching children out in wrongdoing. Try to make double the number of encouraging remarks to critical comments.
- When it is possible, offer children alternatives rather than a straight 'you can't do that'. Be ready to ignore minor misdemeanours, if possible, to avoid a situation in which you seem always to be nagging a particular child. Compromise is a strong option if you choose to offer it, and is not the same as giving in to a child.
- Keep children's troublesome or disruptive behaviour separate from them as individuals. Think of this distinction in your own mind and be prepared to say it out loud – 'I like you, Ramona, but I don't like what you're doing to Freddie.'

- Avoid labels for children, whether these are disrespectful, like 'You're a stupid/selfish/naughty child' or compliments, such as 'What a good little girl.' A positive approach focuses on the child's behaviour at the time, rather than implying that this occasion sums up her entire personality or competence. Never say, 'I won't like you anymore if . . .' A child should never believe that a trusted adult's affection for her can change from moment to moment, depending on what the child does.
- Sometimes young children need to be physically contained within your arms or removed from other children whom they are hurting. Children should neither be dragged, nor hurt through the physical containment. And you should accompany your physical actions with calming words. In such circumstances, adults are using their greater strength appropriately to keep children safe and to help calm them. This is a physical way of reassuring children that you will maintain boundaries when the children have gone beyond their own ability to stop themselves.

A positive approach to children's behaviour is underpinned by a set of values that see adults as having responsibilities towards children as well as rights. A great deal of practice with, and observation of, children in homes and early years settings confirms that the positive, rather than the punitive approach works well and helps children develop as individuals who feel able to guide their own behaviour.

The case against hitting children

If you listen to discussions between adults about children and discipline (in everyday conversation or on the radio or television), you will almost certainly hear adults who believe that it is fine to hit children or are puzzled about what else to do. Some adults express what can only be described as enthusiasm for this kind of punishment and persistently link the right to hit children with the need for discipline. Supporters tend to use the word 'smack' rather than hit, perhaps to avoid facing the contradiction that they are proposing actions against the smaller and younger members of society that would be condemned if used against fellow-adults.

There has been a long tradition in Britain, and other countries, of adults' right to hit children. These beliefs are deep-rooted within culture and are sometimes justified on a religious basis. There is now a strong counter-tradition within work with children, and it is useful for you to understand the opposing views.

The main themes in opposition to hitting children are as follows:

- There is a moral stance that it is wrong to hit children. British society does not, as a whole, approve of adults settling disputes and imposing their wishes through hitting other people. It is unacceptable to treat young children in this way.
- There are many alternatives to hitting when adults need to deal with children's behaviour. Hitting, like any emphasis on punishment, is a negative focus – 'don't' and 'No!' – rather than on what you want the child to do – 'It would be better if you . . .'
- Hitting is far too often a reflection of adults' moods: that they have had enough for today or are embarrassed by a child's public misbehaviour. Children can be given an inconsistent picture by adults who are sometimes cross and hit out, but use different methods on other occasions, which in fact seem similar to the child concerned.
- Children do not like being hit (although some children who are regularly hit may develop a protective shell to give the impression that they do not care). Children tend to focus on the shock and distress of the slap, fierce shove or shake and any lesson about their own behaviour is lost in their reaction to the adult behaviour.
- Hitting gives children the clear message that physical means are an acceptable way to settle arguments or express anger and frustration. They often use this method themselves, either with other children or by hitting the adult in retaliation.
- Supporters of hitting use phrases like 'a gentle smack' or 'loving discipline', but hitting children is rarely calm and you need to challenge the dubious reasoning underlying any claim that it can be an expression of affection.
- Parents who hit must face the problem of what to do if a light 'smack' or 'tap' does nothing to stop a child, or s/he soon returns to the forbidden activity. Parents are tempted to hit harder and longer and can seriously risk losing control.

The Law and Hitting Children

- It has been illegal to use corporal punishment in state schools since the Education Act of 1986 and the majority of independent schools have chosen to remove this option for their staff. Corporal punishment is illegal in residential children's homes under the Children's Homes Regulations 1991.
- Legislation against corporal punishment does not extend to early years centres, nor to the childminding service so, although you may find some child care books which state that hitting children is 'illegal' in all early childhood settings, this statement is inaccurate. Hitting children is

against good practice guidelines and could be grounds for dismissal, but it is not against the law (see 'The situation in early years settings' which follows). Nor does British law prevent parents from hitting their children. Parents are given some leeway for what is described as 'reasonable chastisement', but those who are judged to have overstepped the boundary of acceptable punishment may be prosecuted for assault and causing unnecessary suffering (under the Children and Young Persons Act 1933).

- The British Government, along with many other countries, has signed the United Nations Convention on the Rights of the Child, 1989. Several of the articles within the Convention aim to secure children's right to be protected from physical or mental violence. The UN Committee on the Rights of the Child (which monitors the Convention) has recommended prohibiting physical punishment in families and the active change of social attitudes that support it. The UN Convention is a support to those working against physical punishment but it is not legislation, like the Children Act 1989.

THE SITUATION IN EARLY YEARS SETTINGS

The guidance supporting the Children Act 1989 (Volume Two, relevant to early years settings and childminding) took the stance (in para 6.22) that corporal punishment should not be used in any of the settings within the scope of the guidance. Good practice was already following this recommendation. But guidance is not law, it can be challenged, and this particular paragraph was put the test in 1994 with the case of the London Borough of Sutton versus Anne Hilary Davis (then working as a childminder).

The judgement in this case led to an official circular from the Department of Health which created an option for childminders (but not any other professionals covered by Volume Two of the guidance) to use 'smacking' as a last resort if parents wanted it and the childminder was willing to use such action. The National Childminding Association remains opposed to the use of physical punishment and their good practice guidelines are as supportive of the more positive approaches to discipline as standards for early years settings.

Good practice guidelines for early years settings and playwork centres are consistent in promoting positive methods of handling children's behaviour that do not include physical forms of punishment such as hitting, shoving or shaking children. You are therefore likely to find that a firm condition of your job is that you do not, under any circumstances, hit the children. A constructive policy on behaviour will include the kind of options described on page 159.

A PERSONAL EXAMPLE

My parents disapproved of hitting children; they regarded it as a serious misuse of adult strength. So, it came as a shock to me when my first teacher at primary school (in the 1950s) not only yelled at us, but regularly hit children over the knuckles or on the open palm with a large wooden ruler. I was only ever on the receiving end of this woman's cruel words, but I will never forget watching her hit other five-year-olds, sometimes just for simple mistakes and, in the case of a friend of mine, for writing with his left hand.

In my secondary school (in the 1960s), the religious education teacher had unpredictable outbursts of temper that sometimes led to him hitting pupils very hard round the head. There were many such incidents during my seven years at the school, some bad enough for parents to complain to the headmaster. We finally recognised that this man was never going to be sacked. I later discovered that parents who came to complain were pressed to consider the damage to the school resulting from an assault charge. The man's conduct was further excused on the grounds that he had allegedly been shell-shocked during the Second World War over 20 years previously.

Both my first primary school teacher and the religious education teacher were disliked by the pupils. Neither teacher was respected. They provoked feelings of unease or fear in us because of their unpredictability. But their behaviour was tolerated within schools which also had considerate and talented teachers who did not resort to physical attack, either as a form of punishment or in reaction to some internal fury. As pupils, we reached the conclusion that the actions of these violent teachers fell within what adults regarded as normal behaviour towards children or young people – at an extreme end of the range, perhaps, but acceptable nonetheless.

ACTIVITY

Unless you are above a certain age, you will probably not have any experience of institutions, such as schools, in which the physical punishment of pupils, possibly in public, was a real possibility. Such a situation shaped one's view of adults in authority and of the position of children. Talk with older colleagues or members of your family about their experiences.

1 How did they feel about adults who used physical punishments or threats?
2 What do the memories tell you about a different social era?

Teaching children self-protection

There are a number of positive ways in which you can support all children in learning to keep themselves safe. You cannot protect them completely, but you can help.

Effective programmes to help children learn self-protection draw on different types of resources. Depending on the age of the children, you might use short conversations and small group discussions. Stories, told from books or played out with dolls or puppets, may be another way of communicating simple points to children. Videos can be useful with older children, but the available videos are often not suitable for the younger age range. However, do not depend on resources like books or puppets as a substitute for personal conversations with children. They learn best through talking and listening to a caring adult whom they trust, and who will answer questions now or later and sensitively return to the key ideas at appropriate opportunities in the future. Helping children learn to keep themselves safe is a continuing theme and certainly not something that can be taught in just one or two special sessions during children's early years.

Partnership with parents

You should talk to parents about this area of work. Like any other aspect of your early years curriculum, parents have the right to be informed and consulted about what you are saying to their children and to understand the messages you wish to communicate. For instance, you are not telling their children that it is alright to be rude to strangers, but you *are* explaining that adults do not deserve politeness from children if the adults behave in such a way as to upset, worry or frighten them. Some parents may appreciate being part of discussions and/or will want to read any materials you use.

Themes in keeping safe

Your aim is to help children to develop a self-protective caution without making them think that there is danger lurking around every corner.

Building Confidence in Children

In your role you should be building children's sense of self-confidence and a conviction of their own self-worth. Children learn these feelings as part of a continuing process. Your overall behaviour towards them matters, for instance, as described earlier in the chapter regarding physical care.

Self-confidence is not something that is locked into children's beliefs and behaviour as a result of a few group discussions. For example, a safety discussion with some seven-year-olds might stress the importance of 'telling' rather than keeping quiet about unhappy experiences. However, this message will be undermined if children from the group later find that their attempts to speak up about playground troubles are dismissed by a teacher or playground supervisor as 'telling tales' or the children are told, 'You can sort that out yourself, don't bother me.'

Children need to develop trust in their own feelings. A framework of positive experiences with adults who behave properly will give them a sense of when circumstances are not right or make them uneasy. If you work with older children, perhaps in a school or playwork setting, it is appropriate to take opportunities to affirm and explore children's 'gut' feelings about people. You should not encourage unreasonable criticisms of people or views that seem, after some discussion, to be based on unsupported prejudice, but children's opinions that somebody is 'creepy' or 'not really very nice' are based on their observations.

You might have an open-ended conversation that explores the child's view – 'What makes you say that?' or 'What does he do that you find "creepy"?' Sometimes the explanation will be innocent – perhaps a child has not understood that her uncle leans close because he is hard of hearing. On other occasions there may be aspects of the adult's or young person's behaviour that leave you feeling uneasy and you might explore this further.

RULES WITH FLEXIBILITY

You need to establish guiding rules that do not put children at risk. For instance, young children should not be told that they must be polite to all adults at all times, or given the impression that adults are always in the right. You can encourage courtesy and still help children to understand that some behaviour from adults is inappropriate and removes any adult right to expect politeness from children.

A guideline about 'telling' must not be applied in any way that puts further pressure on children or makes them feel responsible through their silence. Circumstances can combine to make it very difficult for some children to tell about distressing or abusive experiences (see page 93). When a child finally manages to speak out, s/he should not be made to feel uncomfortable about not having told anyone sooner.

You should encourage children to deal non-aggressively with their peers, to speak up rather than hit out in anger and to get help from adults if matters are getting out of hand, but children will not be well protected by an absolute rule that says, 'You must never yell at people or hit them.' Children, especially when they become more independent, may face situations in which talking is not going to help and there is no friendly adult upon whom to call. Children have the right to defend themselves from bullying peers, intimidating older children or adults. They can be taught the strategy of silence and walking away, or running fast, but sometimes an effective defence will include yelling, shoving and hitting out at somebody who will not let the child get away through less noisy or physical ways.

There are Rules for Adults as Well

Children will be learning ground rules for their own behaviour – what is expected, what is not allowed – but they also need to learn that adults cannot simply do as they like: that there are ground rules that apply to adults as well.

- Children can be reassured when caring adults explain that unknown adults are in the wrong if they put children in an awkward position by striking up a conversation with a child who is alone, asking a child for help or pressurising a child to come and look at something. It is not a child's responsibility to sort out the 'bad' strangers from the 'good' ones. On the contrary, it is the responsibility of all adults to behave properly towards children and not to create problems for them.
- Adults, or young people, who are known to a child have no business ill-treating children or pressing them to keep uncomfortable secrets. They have no right to use their adult physical, intellectual or emotional powers to coerce children. That rule holds regardless of whether the children are themselves misbehaving, for instance, by having wandered off from the school group on a trip or having ignored a family rule such as 'don't talk to strangers'. The rule still holds even if children have been coerced into accepting sweets or gifts from the adult or young person.
- Children who are encouraged as a general rule to follow adult requests need to understand that they do not have to obey all adults, especially when what is asked seems wrong or makes the child very uncomfortable. Children need to learn that it is their right to say 'No' and to tell a trusted adult about experiences that they do not like.
- Adults also have responsibilities to create a situation, in schools and other settings, that enables children to follow the rules that the adults have set. For instance, it is unacceptable for the staff of a school or an

after-school club to say 'there's no hitting here', unless the adults step in effectively when some children use physical means to get their own way. Without adult support, the better behaved children may resist hitting back, or get into trouble when they defend themselves. Yet the lesson they are learning is that the strong win out and adults are unfair.

A Framework of Appropriate Behaviour

Over a period of time young children can learn about 'good' and 'bad' physical contact. The earlier section on the physical care of children describes how good practice starts to build this positive framework through children's experience of your behaviour, long before the ideas can make sense to children in words.

Older children are more able to talk around such ideas. Four- and five-year-olds, for instance, can probably grasp the idea of 'good' and 'bad' secrets. 'Good' secrets, perhaps more appropriately called 'surprises', are enjoyable and possibly exciting because they will give pleasure to someone else ('What we've bought Mummy for her birthday'). 'Bad' secrets make children feel uncomfortable or unhappy. They feel they should say something but an adult, or young person, might be pressing them to remain silent against their wishes.

Remain Realistic

Adults, workers or parents need to be cautious and realistic in any work on helping children to keep themselves safe.

Avoid the trap of believing that strangers are the main source of danger to children. Any discussion or leaflet that focuses mainly on 'stranger danger' or not talking to strangers is likely to mislead children. Children are most at risk from adults with whom they are already acquainted – adults either well-known as family or friends or as recognisable local people. Children need to be alerted to adult behaviour and to be wary of adults, whether familiar or unknown, who behave in a way that makes them uneasy or upset. Adults are not the only source of distress or danger to children. They need the confidence to speak up about another child or young person, such as a teenage sitter, who is ill-treating them.

Children should never be left with the impression that they are totally responsible for protecting themselves. Adults carry the main responsibility – both in protecting children and in behaving in a safe and proper way themselves. Children need to feel that they can make some decisions and keep themselves safe, but not that this ability is a burden. Some children have done their best to protect themselves, have said 'No' to an abuser and tried to tell, yet have still experienced abuse. They should never be left with any sense that they failed – the failure and the responsibility rests with the abuser.

You can teach children to yell, push and struggle if they are attacked or grabbed, but do not encourage them in unrealistic estimates of their own physical strength. There is a time to run as fast as possible.

Security in early years settings

Balancing access and security

Any early years team needs to be highly aware of children's safety, to ensure that they cannot walk or crawl off the premises without anybody realising and that visitors to a setting are monitored.

In the second half of the 1990s, several frightening, and sometimes tragic, incidents raised awareness that some mentally disturbed individuals may target settings with children. Nurseries, preschools or primary schools cannot turn themselves into fortresses and it is important to realise that incidents such as the murders at Dunblane primary school are very rare.

The realistic, everyday balance should be between access and security: you want to welcome parents and children into the building, yet avoid making it easy for people who have no business in the centre simply to wander in. You can do this by using the following guidelines:

- Explain how you handle security to parents when they first come with their child.
- You need appropriate front and back door security and for any yard or garden gates. Stress to parents that care over closing doors and gates properly is for the safety of their children.
- At busy times of the day or session, you may need a system in which somebody is always by the door – to greet parents and children, or to say goodbye and courteously check unknown visitors.
- At quieter times of the day, it might be possible to lock the door, so that someone has to answer a knock or bell, or have an entry phone system in operation.
- Any door handles should be out of the reach of younger children. If

you work with older children, for instance in an after-school club, then this could be a good time to teach them about safe behaviour at the door: checking who is there, fetching a worker and not simply opening the door to anyone.

Close circuit television (CCT)

CCT may be considered if your setting is in an area where children may be at risk from local adults, such as one where there is a high proportion of people who suffer from alcoholism or who are mentally unstable. Alternatively you may be in an area with a high burglary rate and so the nursery and its equipment need to be protected.

The choices in CCT are basically between a high profile, visually obvious system or a more covert arrangement in which cameras are hidden in normal equipment such as junction boxes or clocks. The more obvious system can be effective in deterring intruders or thieves, but can be put out of action fairly easily, for instance by spraying the lenses of the camera. If your setting needs CCT, you should get professional advice about the different systems, check your budget and make sure that the system you choose can be easily upgraded or extended if necessary.

CCT security cameras are likely to be positioned at the entrances to your buildings but not in all the group rooms. It has been suggested that this system could be extended to counteract potential abuse by staff. However, CCT is not an effective way to deal with child protection issues and such a system could cause other problems:

- Cameras in every room are not a guaranteed way of catching abusive staff. The few workers who wish to abuse children will avoid the cameras or take children out of the centre to abuse them.
- A CCT system is likely to create an atmosphere of distrust and lack of co-operation from a staff team if it is thought it is being used to spy on them, and is insulting to the majority of staff who aim for good practice.
- Cameras in bathrooms and toilets are a serious breach of privacy for adults or children.

Centre managers and senior workers should be sufficiently visible and present in all parts of the setting to hear or see poor practice; they should not be depending on CCT. Good practice should be established and maintained in any early years setting in the ways discussed in this and other chapters of the book.

There have also been experiments with CCT in a few nurseries where the system is linked to the internet so that working parents or other relatives can log onto the internet and watch their children, feeling part of their day while at their place of work. But this kind of argument is seriously flawed.

- Parents are not spending time with their children or being a genuine part of the child's day; they are watching television.
- There is nothing in the system to ensure that parents or other relatives only watch their own children, or that they do not talk about what they see of another child's frustrations or difficulties.
- The cameras and access on the internet are an infringement of all the children's rights. Just because they are young, children should not be recorded and watched without their informed consent.
- Nurseries have been reassured that paedophiles would not be able to hack into the system and watch children for abusive purposes, but it has been shown that someone with the computer skills and motivation can hack into any system.

Final thoughts

The ideas in this chapter are part of good practice with all babies and children. They form a framework for respectful behaviour towards children and are important regardless of whether your setting ever has to deal with a serious child protection case. Friendly and open communication, a positive approach to children's behaviour and helping children learn to keep themselves safe are all significant parts of the work of an early years setting. Such approaches will not, unfortunately, ensure that children in your care are never abused; there is no guaranteed method for total child protection. Yet good practice will increase the chances for children to speak up rather than keep silent, and to turn to a trusted early years worker to help them deal with and recover from the experience.

Appendix

Name:

Date:

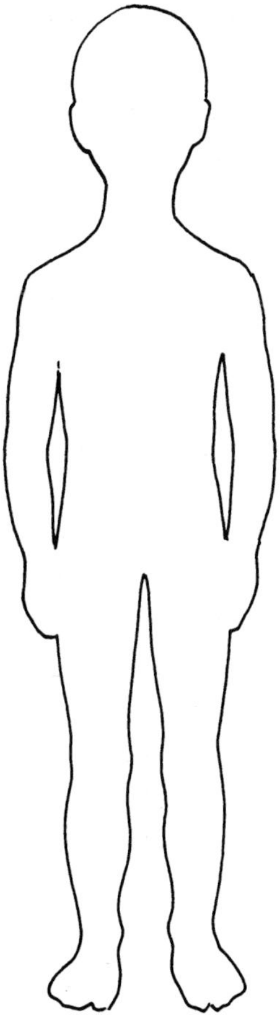

Further reading

Cowley, Liz & Crouch, Maureen (1997) *Managing to change: training materials for staff in centres for young children. Module 5 – Child Protection.* London: National Children's Bureau. Information and exercises for group leaders running workshops on child protection with early years workers.

Department of Health (1982) *Child abuse: a study of inquiry reports 1973–1981* and (1991) *Child abuse: a study of inquiry reports 1980–1989.* London: HMSO. Summaries of reports and implications for good practice in child protection.

Department of Health (1995) *Child protection – messages from research, Studies in Child Protection.* London: HMSO. A summary of 20 studies on child protection in the UK.

Elliott, Michele (1994) *Keeping safe: a practical guide to talking with children.* London: Hodder and Stoughton. Information and advice on helping younger children to keep safe.

Elliott, Michele (1995) *Teenscape: a personal safety programme for teenagers.* London: Health Education Authority. Information and advice on keeping safe, for older children.

Finkelhor, David (1984) *Child sexual abuse: new theory and research.* The Free Press; (1986) *A source book on child sexual abuse.* London: Sage; with Williams, L.M. and Burns, N. (1988) *Nursery Crimes – Sexual Abuse in Nursery Care.* London: Sage. Informative books on research and issues in the area of child sexual abuse.

Gilkes, Julia (1988) 'Coming to terms with sexual abuse: a day care perspective' in *Children in Society,* Vol. 2 (3). How the team of a combined children's centre extended their skills.

Gottman, John (1997) *The heart of parenting: how to raise an emotionally intelligent child.* London: Bloomsbury. Practical suggestions for any adults, not only parents involved with children.

Gulbenkian Foundation (1995) *Report of the Commission on Children and Violence*. The full report and a summary, *Children and Violence*, are available from Calouste Gulbenkian Foundation, 98 Portland Place, London W1N 4ET.

Hewlett, Sylvia Ann (1993) *Child neglect in rich nations*. UNICEF. A sobering reminder that neglect is not restricted to families in poverty. Hewlett considers parents with financial resources but who give little time.

Horwath, Jan & Lawson, Brian (eds) (1996) *Trust betrayed: Munchausen Syndrome by proxy, inter-agency child protection and partnership with families*. London: National Children's Bureau. Provides information on the diagnosis of MSBP and the work of the different professions involved in this aspect of physical child abuse.

Jensen, Jytte Juul (1995) *Men as workers in childcare services*. European Commission Network on Childcare. Consideration of the many issues that are raised when men are part of an early years team, with descriptions of Scandinavian centres.

Kelley, Susan (1994) 'Abuse of children in day care centres: characteristics and consequences' in *Child Abuse Review*, Vol. 3. A descriptive account of features of abuse centred on early years settings.

La Fontaine, J. (1994) *The extent and nature of organised and ritual sexual abuse: research findings*. London: HMSO. A balanced consideration of the objective evidence on the existence of organised sexual abuse or satanic group rituals in child abuse.

Lau, Annie, 'Cultural perspectives and significant harm: its assessment and treatment' in Adcock, Margaret, White, Richard and Hollows, Anne (1991) *Significant harm: its management and outcome*. Significant Publications. Practical issues when families and professionals do not share a cultural background.

Leach, Penelope (1992) *Young children under stress* (National Early Years Network – Starting Points No. 6). The different sources of stress on children and what can be done to relieve them.

Leach, Penelope (1997) *Getting positive about discipline: a guide for today's parents* and *Why speak out against smacking: questions and answers from the physical punishment debate*. Essex: Barnados. Ideas and practical issues for workers as well as parents.

Lindon, Jennie (1997) *Working with young children*. London: Hodder and Stoughton. Good practice, including observation and record keeping, a positive approach to children's behaviour and partnership with parents.

Lindon, Jennie & Lindon, Lance (1997) *Working together for young children: a guide for managers and staff*. Basingstoke: Macmillan. Teamwork, dealing with conflict and partnership with parents – issues in general good practice, as well as child protection.

National Children's Bureau Highlight series:
1991: *Children as witnesses* (no. 104)
1992: *Children as witnesses – Scotland* (no. 112)
1993: *Child sexual abuse* (no. 119)
1995: *Children and domestic violence* (no. 139)
1997: *Guardians ad litem and reporting officers* (no. 147)
1997: *Parental psychiatric disorder and child maltreatment. Part I: Context and historical overview* (no. 148)
1997: *Parental psychiatric disorder and child maltreatment. Part II: Extent and nature of association* (no. 149)
1997: *The Children (Scotland) Act 1995* (no. 152)
1997: *The Children (Northern Ireland) Order* (no. 153)
The NCB Highlight series is presented as single sheets, printed on both sides. They offer useful, short summaries of research and issues in a given area. (The NCB's address can be found on page 180.)

NCH Action for Children:
(Undated) *Child abuse* and *Child sexual abuse factsheets*
(1994) *The hidden victims: children and domestic violence – summary report*
(1994) *Children sexually abusing other children: the last taboo? – summary report*
(1997) *Making a difference: working with women and children experiencing domestic violence*
NCH Action for Children publishes factsheets, summaries and reports that provide useful information in a concise format (address on page 180).

National Society for the Prevention of Cruelty to Children (NSPCC) (1992) *Child protection procedures – what they mean for your family*. London: NSPCC. Written by the Family Rights Group, this useful publication is organised as a series of questions that parents might ask about the child protection process.

NSPCC (undated) *Happy children – sad children: all about children's feelings.* London: NSPCC. This publication could guide your work but is designed so that parents or older children can read it themselves.

NSPCC (1995) *The abuse of children in day care settings: conference report of June 1994.* London: NSPCC National Training Centre. Practical issues of facing the reality of child abuse in a day care setting.

NSPCC:
(1996) *Listening to children: a guide for parents*
(1996) *Stress: a guide for parents*
(1997) *Protecting children from sexual abuse in the community: a guide for parents and carers*
(1997) *Stop the violence: a guide to keeping children safe*
Booklets useful for early years workers or to make available for parents.

Newell, Peter (1992) *Children are people too: the case against physical punishment.* London: EPOCH. Putting the case for respectful treatment of children, including the freedom from being hit or physically punished in other ways.

Ofshe, Richard & Walters, Ethan (1995) *Making monsters: false memories, psychotherapy and sexual hysteria.* Andre Deutsch. An account of the dangers when professionals lose objectivity and become so convinced of the existence of a problem that they risk creating one.

Ruxton, Sandy (1992) *What's he doing at the family centre: the dilemmas of men who care for children* (NCH Action for Children Research report). London: NCH. Discussion of the issues of male workers in a predominantly female job, illustrated with examples of men who have worked in different early years centres.

Schonveld, Anne (1995) *Schools and child protection: a training handbook for designated teachers.* Community Education Development Centre. A practical handbook with information and training materials relevant to schools in their work with children and young people.

Slaby, Ronald, Roedell, Wendy, Arezzo, Diana & Hendrix, Kate (1995) *Early violence prevention: tools for teachers of young children.* National Association for the Education of Young Children – available from the National Early Years Network, London (address on page 180). Suggestions for guiding children away from aggressive strategies in dealing with their problems and towards prosocial behaviour.

Smith, David R. (1993) *Safe from harm: a code of practice for safeguarding the welfare of children in voluntary organisations.* London: The Home Office. A comprehensive list of procedures and guidance in child protection, with examples of policies.

Wilson, Avril & Joseph, Yvonne (1996) *Recognising child abuse: a guide for early years workers.* London: National Early Years Network – Starting Points No. 6. A short practical book highlighting issues and good practice for early years workers in different settings.

Wilson, Melba (1993) *Crossing the boundary: black women survive incest.* London: Virago. Personal experience and professional analysis of the issues arising from sexual abuse in African-Caribbean and African-American communities.

You will sometimes find relevant articles in *Nursery World*, *Co-ordinate* (National Early Years Network) and *Children UK* (National Children's Bureau). Articles on research and practice appear regularly in *The Child Abuse Review*, the journal of the British Association for the Study and Prevention of Child Abuse and Neglect.

Useful addresses

A number of useful organisations are listed below. Most of them do not specifically deal with child abuse but deal with issues related to the broader context of the welfare of children, young people and their families.

Barnados is a national children's charity which runs a wide range of projects for children, young people and their families. The main office is at Tanners Lane, Barkingside, Ilford, Essex 1G6 1QG, tel: 020 8550 8822. Their publications are available from Child Care Publications, Barnardos Trading, Paycocke Road, Basildon, Essex SS14 3DR, tel: 01268 520224.

Children's Legal Centre offers publications on the law as it affects children and young people and operates an advice line on legal issues. The centre is at the University of Essex, Wivenhoe Park, Colchester, Essex CO4 3SQ, tel: 01206 873820.

Cry-sis offers support to parents with babies who cry incessantly or with older children with emotional difficulties. The organisation offers information and a helpline. Contact them at BM Cry-sis, London WC1N 3XX, tel: 020 7404 5011.

Early Education (formerly BAECE) offers advice, conferences and practical publications on all aspects of early learning for young children. They can be reached at 136 Cavell Street, London E1 2JA, tel: 020 7539 5400.

End Physical Punishment of Children (EPOCH) aims to end all physical punishment of children through legal reform and re-education of adults. EPOCH provides advice for parents and carers through publications. The organisation can be contacted at 77 Holloway Road, London N7 8J6, tel: 020 7700 0627.

Family Rights Group offers a telephone advice service for families whose children are involved with social services. They can be contacted at 18 Ashwin Street, London E8 3DL, tel: 020 7249 0008 for advice and 020 7923 2628 for enquiries.

Home-Start UK offers practical help for families under stress (not necessarily at risk of abuse). Trained volunteers are sent into homes to offer regular help and support. The national office is at 2 Salisbury Road, Leicester LE1 7QR, tel: 0116 233 9955, where you will be put in touch with the nearest local scheme.

Kidscape offers publications and training courses about child abuse, teaching children self-protection and dealing with bullying. The organisation is at 152 Buckingham Palace Road, London SW10 9TR, tel: 020 7730 3300.

NCH Action for Children runs projects and family centres for children and their parents and publishes books and leaflets. The main office is at 85 Highbury Road, London N5 1UD, tel: 020 7226 2033.

National Children's Bureau (NCB) has a wide range of projects and publications relevant to children and their families. The Bureau is at 8 Wakley Street, London EC1V 7QE, tel: 020 7843 6000. The Bureau has several different units, including the Early Childhood Unit (tel: 020 7843 6064) and the Family Support and Child Protection Unit (tel: 020 7843 6097). The NCB works in partnership with *Children in Scotland/Clann An Alba* (Princes House, 5 Shandwick Place, Edinburgh EH2 4RG, tel: 0131 228 8484) and *Children in Wales/Plant yng Nghymru* (25 Windsor Place, Cardiff CF1 3BZ, tel: 029 2034 2434).

National Early Years Network (NEYN) focuses on issues that affect all the different types of early years centres. The NEYN runs seminars and workshops, and publishes the *Starting Points* series. NEYN can be contacted at 77 Holloway Road, London N7 8JZ, tel: 020 7607 9573.

National Private Day Nurseries Association (NPDNA) is an organisation for the private sector in day care and education. The NPDNA organises conferences, local and national training and contact with other private nurseries. Contact them at Portland House, 55 New Hey Road, Lindley, Huddersfield HD3 4AL, tel: 01484 546502.

National Society for the Prevention of Cruelty to Children (NSPCC) is the only national voluntary organisation authorised by law to take legal proceedings to protect a child from abuse. The NSPCC has local child protection teams and assessment services and offers publications and training. The national office is at 42 Curtain Road, London EC2A 3NH, tel: 020 7825 2500. The *Irish Society for the Prevention of Cruelty to Children (ISPCC)* is at

20 Molesworth Street, Dublin 2, tel: 010 35316794944. The *Royal Scottish Society for the Prevention of Cruelty to Children (RSSPCC)* is at Melville House, 41 Polworth Terrace, Edinburgh E11 1NV, tel: 0131 337 8539.

Parents Anonymous, 6 Manor Gardens, London N7 6LA, tel: 020 7263 8918. The organisation runs a helpline for parents who are tempted to abuse or are abusing their children.

Parentline puts parents in touch with a national network of organisations, helplines and drop-in centres. You can contact them at Endway House, The Endway, Hadleigh, Essex SS7 2AN, tel: 01702 559900.

Pre-school Learning Alliance (PLA) is the organisation for playgroups – many of which are now known as preschools. The PLA offer support, training and a wide range of publications (relevant for all early years workers). The PLA can be contacted at 69 Kings Cross Road, London WC1X 9LL, tel: 020 7833 0991.

If you are searching for additional organisations relevant to children and their families, then *Organisations concerned with young children and their families* (1995), jointly published by the National Children's Bureau and the National Early Years Network is a very useful resource.

Links to child care qualifications

This book will support your study in the following qualifications:

NVQs/SVQs in Early Years Care and Education

LEVEL 2

Unit C4 – Support children's social and emotional development

LEVEL 3

Unit C5 – Promote children's social and emotional development
Unit C15 – Contribute to the protection of children from abuse

NVQ/SVQ in Playwork

LEVEL 2

Unit C36 – Support the protection of children from abuse
Unit PA1 – Contribute to positive relationships with children and their parents/carers

LEVEL 3

Unit D27 – Promote children's social and emotional development
Unit H4 – Support the protection of children from abuse

CACHE courses

CERTIFICATE IN CHILD CARE AND EDUCATION

Core module 3 – Child safety
Core module 9 – Emotional and social development

NNEB DIPLOMA IN NURSERY NURSING

Module F – Emotional and social development
Module N – Child protection

ADVANCED DIPLOMA IN CHILD CARE AND EDUCATION

Module 3 – Feelings and relationships
Module 9 – Children and families under stress
Module 14 – Child protection

BTEC National

Childhood Studies (nursery nursing) – module on Practices in Child Care

Index